THE
NEW
FIRST
AID IN
ENGLISH

SECOND
EDITION

Angus Maciver

D1340130

HODDER
GIBSON
AN HACHETTE UK COMPANY

Preface

Used wherever the English language is spoken or taught, this book has proved invaluable in class and as a reference book, both to native English speakers and to students of English as a second language.

For all such students *The New First Aid in English Second Edition* is an essential companion, helpful alike in cases of difficulty with vocabulary, spelling, syntax, idiom and correct usage.

Students of English as a second language have found it of immense value both as an aid to conversation and as a rapid revision course before taking examinations.

A separate answer book is available:

Answers to the New First Aid in English Second Edition (ISBN 978 0 340 88288 7)

Orders: please contact Bookpoint Ltd, 130 Milton Park, Abingdon, Oxon OX14 4SB. Telephone: +44 (0)1235 827720. Fax: +44 (0)1235 400454. Lines are open from 9.00 to 5.00, Monday to Saturday, with a 24-hour message answering service. You can also order through our website www.hodderheadline.co.uk

© Angus Maciver 1938, 1956, 1986, 2004

First published 1938 by Hodder Gibson, an Hachette UK company,
338 Euston Road
London NW1 3BH
First Aid in English first published 1938
The New First Aid in English first published 1956
The New First Aid in English Revised first published 1986 and reprinted 19 times
This second edition first published 2004
Impression number   14
Year   2010

Typeset in 11/14pt Garamond ITC by Fakenham Photosetting Limited, Fakenham, Norfolk

Printed and bound in India.

A CIP catalogue record for this title is available from the British Library

ISBN 978 0 340 88287 0

Contents

Contents

The English Language

English is an international language. It is written and spoken all over the world. It is spoken in a variety of accents – English, American, West Indian, Indian – but its grammar and most of its vocabulary remain the same no matter where it is used. The English used in a newspaper like Jamaica's *Daily Gleaner* is much the same as the English in *The New York Times*, *The Times of India* or *The Guardian*.

English has borrowed words from almost every other language. Look at these examples:

card (French) piano (Italian) fox (German) bungalow (Hindi)
canoe (Carib) dictator (Latin) admiral (Arabic)

English has its origins in northern Europe. Its grammar shows its roots in languages like German and Dutch. A typical English sentence has a Noun or Noun Phrase (Subject) followed by a Verb and another Noun or Noun Phrase (Object), e.g.

The fat man drove a big red car.
  [Subject] [Verb] [Object]

Parts of Speech

English words can be classified into different parts of speech according to the part they play in making sentences in the language. Thus, all English words fall into eight main categories:

Nouns
A noun is the name of a person, animal, place or thing, e.g. John, tiger, school, kettle, honesty.

Verbs
A verb may be said to be a "doing" word, e.g. eat, think, write.

Pronouns
A pronoun is a word which takes the place of a noun, e.g. he, she, it.

Adjectives
An adjective describes a noun or a pronoun, e.g. good, fine, red.

Adverbs
An adverb generally modifies a verb, e.g. quietly, here, suddenly.

Prepositions
A preposition shows the relation between one thing and another, e.g. against, for, with.

Conjunctions
A conjunction is a word used for joining words and clauses, e.g. and, but.

Exclamations or Interjections
An exclamation or interjection expresses sudden emotion, e.g. Oh! Hello! Stop!

When we wish to express a thought we use words grouped together in a certain order so that we convey a sensible, definite meaning. This combination of words is termed a **sentence**. In conversation or writing, sentences should always be used in order that the hearer or reader may clearly understand the meaning.

Number

Most nouns have a **Singular** form used to denote **one** person or thing and a different **Plural** form denoting **more** than **one**. Pronouns and verbs also have different singular and plural forms.

Singular	Plural	Singular	Plural
box	boxes	child	children
brush	brushes	foot	feet
fox	foxes	goose	geese
gas	gases	man	men
glass	glasses	mouse	mice
watch	watches	ox	oxen
army	armies	tooth	teeth
city	cities	woman	women
fly	flies		
lady	ladies		
calf	calves		
half	halves	brother	{ brothers / brethren }
knife	knives		
leaf	leaves	person	{ people / persons }
life	lives		
loaf	loaves	fish	{ fishes / fish }
shelf	shelves		
thief	thieves	genius	{ geniuses / genii }
wolf	wolves		
chief	chiefs	halo	{ halos / haloes }
dwarf	dwarfs, dwarves		
hoof	hoofs, hooves	penny	{ pennies / pence }
reef	reefs		
roof	roofs		
cargo	cargoes		
echo	echoes		
hero	heroes		
wife	wives	cod	cod
potato	potatoes	deer	deer
banjo	banjos	dozen	dozen
day	days	grouse	grouse
sky	skies	salmon	salmon
piano	pianos	sheep	sheep
solo	solos	swine	swine
valley	valleys	trout	trout

Singular	Plural	Singular	Plural
brother-in-law	brothers-in-law	bye-law	bye-laws
by-way	by-ways	mouse-trap	mouse-traps
cupful	cupfuls	passer-by	passers-by
hanger-on	hangers-on	son-in-law	sons-in-law
man-of-war	men-of-war	spoonful	spoonfuls

The following words have no singular:

bellows, billiards, gallows, measles, pincers, pliers, scissors, shears, spectacles, thanks, tidings, tongs, trousers, tweezers, victuals.

Exercises   on Number

1. **State the plural of:**

   loaf, man-of-war, piano, sheep, foot, echo, penny, life, deer, ox.

2. **Give the singular of:**

   ladies, thieves, geese, trout, passers-by, mice, knives, teeth, boxes.

3. **Fill in the blank spaces – the singular or plural form – as required:**

army	_____	son-in-law	_____
_____	roofs	cargo	_____
_____	women	_____	children
cupful	_____		flies
swine	_____	halo	_____
dwarf	_____		potatoes

4. **Give the plural of:**

   police-constable, daughter-in-law, step-child, looker-on, housewife, fireman.

5. **Give the singular of:**

   glasses, hoofs, heroes, feet, pence, fish, shelves, cities, men, leaves.

Exercises on Number continued

6. Change all **Singulars** into **Plurals**.

a) I heard the echo in the cave.
b) The lady spoke to the child.
c) The boy went for a loaf.
d) The man fed the calf.
e) The mouse ran into a hole.
f) The knife was lying on the table.
g) The fisherman caught a trout.
h) The dwarf gave him a stick.
i) The ship struck the reef.
j) My foot troubled me.
k) It was a man's boot.
l) The burglar tried to rob my shop.
m) The prisoner says that he is innocent.
n) The girl's hat was on the peg.
o) The boy robbed a bird's nest.
p) His tooth hurt him badly.
q) The farmer ploughs his field.
r) The horse is eating a raw carrot.
s) The child cried because he was tired.
t) This is the house in which I stay.

7. Change all **Singulars** into **Plurals** and **Verbs** into the **Past Tense**.

a) The rabbit runs from the dog.
b) The girl wears a blue dress.
c) The sailor swims to his ship.
d) The woman catches the goose.
e) The man shoots the deer.
f) The ox eats the potato.
g) The lady prefers the rose.
h) The sheep runs in the valley.
i) Her foot is badly cut.
j) The thief steals the valuable bag.
k) The child runs to the table.
l) He is a man of means.
m) I keep the bird in a cage.
n) He writes my name.
o) She tells me so.
p) He has a sharp knife.
q) She takes his pencil.
r) The old woman sits on that seat.
s) The man walks slowly to his job.
t) The mouse scampers from the cat.

Gender

Nouns and pronouns belong to one or another of four **genders** in grammar. These are:

1. Masculine – words denoting male creatures, e.g. boy, king.

2. Feminine – words denoting female creatures, e.g. girl, queen.

3. Common – words denoting creatures of either sex, e.g. child, owner.

4. Neuter – words denoting things of neither sex, e.g. house, box.

Masculine	Feminine	Masculine	Feminine
abbot	abbess	bachelor	spinster
actor	actress	beau	belle
baron	baroness	boy	girl
count	countess	bridegroom	bride
duke	duchess	brother	sister
emperor	empress	earl	countess
enchanter	enchantress	father	mother
god	goddess	fiancé	fiancée
heir	heiress	friar	nun
host	hostess	gentleman	lady
lion	lioness	he	she
marquis	marchioness	hero	heroine
master	mistress	him	her
mayor	mayoress	husband	wife
priest	priestess	king	queen
prince	princess	lad	lass
male	female	lord	lady
man	woman	masseur	masseuse
monk	nun	Mr	Mrs
nephew	niece		

Masculine	Feminine	Masculine	Feminine
shepherd	shepherdess	sir	madam
sorcerer	sorceress	son	daughter
steward	stewardess	Sultan	Sultana
tiger	tigress	tutor	governess
widower	widow	uncle	aunt
waiter	waitress	wizard	witch
boar	sow	billy-goat	nanny-goat
buck	doe	buck-rabbit	doe-rabbit
bull	cow	bull-calf	cow-calf
bullock	heifer	cock-sparrow	hen-sparrow
cock	hen	father-in-law	mother-in-law
colt	filly	grandfather	grandmother
dog	bitch	headmaster	headmistress
drake	duck	he-goat	she-goat
gander	goose	landlord	landlady
hart	hind	male-child	female-child
hound	brach	manservant	maidservant
ram	ewe	postman	postwoman
sire	dam	postmaster	postmistress
stag	hind	son-in-law	daughter-in-law
stallion	mare	stepfather	stepmother
steer	heifer	stepson	stepdaughter
Alexander	Alexandra	John	Joan
Cecil	Cecilia	Joseph	Josephine
Charles	Charlotte	Oliver	Olive
Christian	Christina	Patrick	Patricia
Clarence	Clara	Paul	Pauline
Francis	Frances	Robert	Roberta
George	Georgina	Victor	Victoria
Henry	Henrietta	William	Wilhelmina

Common gender words denote creatures of **either sex** and the same word may be used **both of male and of female**, e.g.

adult, animal, baby, bird, cat, cattle, child, companion, comrade, cousin, darling, dear, deer, fowl, friend, guardian, guest, infant, juvenile, orphan, owner, parent, passenger, pig, pupil, relation, relative, scholar, sheep, singer, student, swan, teacher, tourist, traveller, visitor.

Neuter gender words denote **things without life or sex**, e.g.

bag, boots, box, bread, butter, chair, chalk, chimney, church, cocoa, coffee, desk, dishes, door, floor, house, jacket, jotter, kettle, knife, mirror, pencil, pillow, ruler, school, seat, stairs, street, table.

Exceptions

We often speak of lifeless things as being male or female, e.g.

Sailors refer to their ships as **she**.
Motorists refer to their cars as **she**.
Pilots refer to their aeroplanes as **she**.

Names of things that suggest **power** or **dignity** are spoken of as if they were **masculine**, e.g.

Time, Winter, Mountains, Sun, Death.

Names of things that suggest **beauty** or **gentleness** are spoken of as if they were **feminine**, e.g.

Spring, Moon, Liberty, Peace, Nature.

On the other hand, we sometimes refer to a cat, dog, horse and other animals as **it**.

Exercises on Gender

1. **Give the feminine of:**

   heir, monk, stallion, nephew, gander, waiter, sir, ram, hero, bachelor.

2. **Give the masculine of:**

   witch, filly, cow, maidservant, wife, duck, bride, duchess, aunt.

Exercises   on Gender continued

3. State the gender of:

lion, cousin, mistress, friend, pencil, steward, sister, book, child.

4. Give the feminine of:

headmaster, step-father, son-in-law, billy-goat.

5. Fill in blank spaces – the masculine or feminine form – as required:

a)	lion	_____	f)	bull	_____	
b)	_____	lady	g)	grandfather	_____	
c)	_____	governess	h)	_____	hind	
d)	male	_____	i)	_____	widow	
e)	actor	_____	j)	tomcat	_____	

6. Give the corresponding feminine of:

Joseph, Henry, Patrick, Charles, John.

7. Change all masculines into corresponding feminines:
a) The bridegroom is my nephew.
b) My landlord is a widower.
c) The wizard spoke to the prince.
d) The Duke chatted to the man.
e) The heir to the estate is a bachelor.
f) "No, sir," he replied.
g) The waiter served his own brother.
h) "He was indeed a hero," said the emperor.
i) The lion sprang at the colt.
j) The master gave instructions to the manservant.
k) "Well!" said his grandfather, "How are you, my little lad?"
l) The steward brought a glass of water to my uncle, who was seasick.
m) The host was extremely puzzled by the twin brothers.
n) The son of a king is termed a prince.
o) The mayor talked to the father of the little boy.

Exercises — on Gender continued

p) The old man told his shepherd to search for the ram.
q) His father-in-law spoke to the manager.
r) He was the stepson of an elderly count.
s) The headmaster rebuked the boy for his conduct.
t) He owned a pet gander called Joseph.

Families

Parents		Young
father	mother	baby or child
king	queen	prince or princess
man	woman	baby or child
bear	she-bear	cub
billy-goat	nanny-goat	kid
boar (pig)	sow	piglet
buck (deer)	hind	fawn
buck (hare)	doe	leveret
buck (rabbit)	doe	rack
bull (cattle)	cow	calf
bull (elephant)	cow	calf
bull (seal)	cow	calf
bull (whale)	cow	calf
cob (swan)	pen	cygnet
cock (fowl)	hen	chicken
cock (pigeon)	hen	squab
dog	bitch	pup
dog (fox)	vixen	cub
drake	duck	duckling
eagle	eagle	eaglet
gander	goose	gosling
hawk	bowess	bowet
hold (ferret)	jill	hob
leopard	leopardess	cub
lion	lioness	cub

Parents		Young
owl	owl	owlet
ram (sheep)	ewe	lamb
stag (red deer)	hind	fawn
stallion (horse)	mare	foal
tiercel (peregrine)	falcon	eyas
tiger	tigress	cub
tomcat	queen or tabby cat	kitten
wolf	she-wolf	cub

Adult	Young	Adult	Young
bee	grub	moth	caterpillar
bird	nestling	salmon	parr
butterfly	caterpillar	toad	tadpole
eel	elver	trout	fry
frog	tadpole	wasp	grub

Exercises on Families

1. Name the young of:

fox, eagle, goose, sheep, pig, goat, cow, horse.

2. Name the parent of:

fawn, pup, cygnet, chicken, leveret, kitten, owlet, duckling.

3. Fill in the blank spaces – the name of parent or young – as required:

wolf	_____	_____	kid
_____	foal	bear	_____
sow	_____	_____	lamb
_____	gosling	eagle	_____

4. Give the names for:

a young salmon, a young eel, a young trout, a young bird.

Traditional Homes

Person	Home	Creature	Home
Aborigine	humpy	badger	sett, earth
convict	prison	bear	den
Inuit	igloo	beaver	lodge
king	palace	bee	hive
lumberjack	log-cabin	bird	nest
man/woman	house	cow	byre, cowshed
Maori	whare	dog	kennel
minister	manse	eagle	eyrie
monk	monastery	fowl	coop
noble	castle	fox	earth, lair
Native American	wigwam or tepee	hare	form
		horse	stable
nun	convent	lion	lair, den
parson	parsonage	mouse	hole, nest
pioneer	wagon	pig	sty
priest (eastern)	temple	otter	holt
prisoner	cell	owl	barn, tree
soldier	barracks or camp	rabbit (tame)	hutch
		rabbit (wild)	burrow, warren
Swiss (herdsman)	chalet	sheep	pen, fold
traveller	caravan	snail	shell
vicar	vicarage	spider	web
Zulu	kraal	squirrel	drey
		tiger	lair
		wasp	nest, vespiary

Exercises on Traditional Homes

1. **Name the homes of:**

    king, minister, lumberjack, parson, monk, Native American, Inuit, Zulu.

2. **Whom would you expect to find living in the following?**

    convent, palace, barracks, cell, vicarage.

3. **Name the homes of the following creatures:**

    cow, dog, eagle, bee, pig, fox, wild rabbit, wasp, bird, lion.

4. **What creatures live in the following places?**

    drey, hutch, pen, form, stable.

Names

First or Christian or Given Names: names given to children at their christening, baptism or naming ceremony, usually different for boys and girls. Many are names of Biblical characters and ancient heroes and heroines. Most have shortened forms – so-called 'pet' names.

Male First Names

Adam
Ahmed
Alan
Alfred (Alf, Fred)
Ali
Andrew (Andy, Drew)
Anthony (Tony)
Antonio
Ben
Brian
Carlton
Charles (Charlie)
Christopher (Chris, Kit)
Daniel (Dan, Danny)
David (Dave)
Dev
Edward (Ed, Ned, Ted)
Errol
Ethan
Francis (Frank)
Garry
George
Gordon
Harry
Hugh (Hughie)
Jack
James (Jamie, Jim, Jimmy)
John (Johnny)
Joseph (Joe, Joey)
Joshua (Josh)
Laurence (Larry)
Lewis
Liam
Luke
Marcus

Matthew (Matt)
Michael (Mike, Mick)
Mohammed
Nelson
Oliver
Patrick (Pat, Paddy)
Peter (Pete)
Philip (Phil)
Ranjit
Ricardo
Richard (Dick, Richie)
Robert (Bob, Bobby, Robin, Bert)
Samuel (Sam, Sammy)
Shiva
Stephen (Steve)
Vishnu
Wesley (Wes)
William (Bill, Will)

Female First Names

Alice
Amanda (Mandy)
Amy
Andrea
Angela (Angie)
Ann (Annie, Nan, Nancy)
Barbara (Babs)
Bernice
Caitlin
Catherine (Cathie, Kate, Kitty)
Cecilia (Cis, Cissie)
Charlotte
Chloe
Christina (Chrissie, Tina)
Devi
Dorothy (Dot, Dolly)
Eleanor (Ella, Ellie, Nell)

Female First Names

Elizabeth (Betty, Liz, Lizzie)	Margaret (Marjory, Maggie, Peggy)
Emily	Maria
Emma	Marion
Fiona	Mary (May, Molly)
Florence (Flo, Flossie)	Megan
Grace	Mia
Hannah	Mina
Helen (Nell)	Olivia
Holly	Rebecca (Becky)
Jane (Jean, Jeanie)	Rose (Rosie)
Janet (Jenny, Jess, Jessie)	Sameera
Jessica (Jess)	Sarah (Sally, Sadie)
Judith (Judy)	Sophie
Julia (Julie)	Susan (Sue, Susie)
Katherine (Kathy, Katie)	Victoria (Vicky)
Kim	Violet (Vi)
Lauren	Winifred
Lilian (Lily)	Yasmin
Lucy	Yvonne
	Zoë

Many first names have a meaning in Hebrew, Greek, Latin, Gaelic or Old English e.g.
Amanda – lovable; Katherine – pure; Charles – manly; Christopher – carrier of Christ;
Clement – merciful; Cyril – lordly; Donald – world chief; Ethel – noble; Fiona – fair;
Hilary – cheerful; Margaret – pearl; Peter – rock; Philip – lover of horses;
Stephen – crown; Zoë – life.

Surnames: a child's last name is usually the family name of the child's father. On marriage
a woman normally takes the surname of her husband, though nowadays some do not.
Note, however, that in China the surname is not the last, but the first name (see page 14).

Many surnames were formed as shown below:

◆ From **Occupations**: Archer, Baker, Clark, Cook, Farmer, Fisher, Hunter, Mason,
Miller, Porter, Shepard, Slater, Smith, Taylor, Wright.

◆ From **Places**: Burns, Cape, England, Forest, Ford, Hall, Hamilton, Hill, Lake,
London, Mills, Scotland, Stirling, Wells, Woods.

◆ From **Animals**: Bullock, Fox, Hare, Hart, Hogg, Lamb, Lyon, Wolfe.

◆ From **Birds**: Drake, Nightingale, Peacock, Swan, Wren.

◆ From **Colours**: Black, Blue, Brown, Grey, Green, White.

◆ From **Qualities of Mind or Body**: Blyth, Bright, Gay, Good, Hardie, Little, Merry,
Noble, Short, Small, Smart, Strong, Young.

Names in other countries

In Kenya the word **arap** in a name means "son of", e.g. the former President of Kenya is named Daniel Toroitich arap Moi. Similarly in other districts the Kikuyu, Kamba, Meru and Embu tribes use **wa** meaning "son of" or "daughter of".

In Arabic-speaking countries, parents are often known by their relation to their children. Thus, Abu means "father of"; Oom means "mother of". Thus:

Abu Ahmed = the father of Ahmed
Oom Ali = the mother of Ali

In a similar way, children are often known by their relation to their parents by the use of **bin** (son of) and **binte** (daughter of). Thus:

Ahmed bin Fuad = Ahmed, son of Faud
Faridah binte Hussein = Faridah, daughter of Hussein

In Singapore Indian names would include **S/O** (Son of) or **D/O** (Daughter of), e.g. Selvarajoo S/O Velu or Saraswethy D/O Rajoo.

Chinese names are written with the family name first, e.g. the Prime Minister of Singapore is the Honourable Goh Chok Tong, Goh being the family name. An interesting fact about Chinese names is that the second name denotes the generation. As an example take the name Tan Wu Cheng. Tan is the family name, Wu the generation name and Cheng the personal name. Should Mr Tan have a brother or brothers they will all bear the same family name, Tan, followed by the generation name Wu followed by their own personal name, Cheng or Ling or any other given name.

In Iceland the boy or girl would, in addition to their own personal name, be given their father's name with the addition of son or daughter, e.g. Magnus' father was called John so Magnus Johnson would be the boy's name.

Group Terms or Collections

Animate

an army of ants
an army of soldiers
a band of musicians
a bench of bishops
a bench of magistrates
a bevy of ladies
a board of directors
a brood of chickens
a building of rooks
a choir of singers
a class of pupils, students
a company of actors
a covey of grouse
a crew of sailors
a drove of cattle
a flock of birds
a flock of sheep
a gaggle of geese
a gang of labourers
a gang of thieves
a group of friends
a herd of buffaloes

a herd of cattle
a host of angels
a litter of cubs
a litter of pups
a nest of rabbits
a pack of rascals
a pack of wolves
a plague of insects
a plague of locusts
a pride of lions
a school of whales
a shoal of herring
a staff of servants
a staff of teachers
a stud of horses
a swarm of bees
a swarm of insects
a team of horses
a team of oxen
a team of players
a troop of monkeys
a troupe of dancers

Inanimate

a bale of cotton, wool
a batch of bread
a bouquet of flowers
a bunch of grapes
a bundle of rags
a chest of drawers
a clump of trees
a cluster of diamonds, stars
a clutch of eggs
a collection of pictures
a crate of fruit
a fleet of cars, ships
a flight of aeroplanes, steps

a forest of trees
a hail of fire
a hedge of bushes
a library of books
a pack of cards
a rope of pearls
a set of china, clubs, tools
a sheaf of corn
a stack of hay
a string of beads
a suit of clothes
a suite of furniture, rooms
a tuft of grass

15

People

at a concert	audience
in church	congregation
in the street	crowd, throng
in a riot	mob
in a rowdy scene	rabble
at a sporting event	crowd

Less Common Examples

a baren of mules	a rag of colts
a bevy of quails	a siege of herons
a cast of hawks	a skulk of foxes
a cete of badgers	a sloth of bears
a clowder of cats	a smuck of jellyfish
a covert of coots	a stand of plovers
a down of hares	a string of horses
a fall of woodcocks	a tribe of goats
a field of runners	a watch of nightingales
a flight of doves	a wisp of snipe
a flight of swallows	
a gang of elks	a budget of papers
a gathering of clans	a bunch of bananas
a herd of antelopes	a cast of flowerpots
a herd of cranes	a crate of crockery
a host of sparrows	a fusillade of shots
a kindle of kittens	a galaxy of stars
a labour of moles	a group of islands
a leap of leopards	a nest of machine guns
a muster of peacocks	a peal of bells
a nest of mice	a punnet of strawberries
a nide of pheasants	a sheaf of arrows
a pace of asses	a shock of wheat
a paddling of ducks	a skein of silk
a posse of sheriff's men	a skein of wool
	a truss of hay

Exercises   on Group Terms or Collections

1. A number of sheep together is called a flock. What name is given to a number of:
   choir *pack* *swarm* *gang* *litter*
   singers, ships, wolves, trees, bees, whales, thieves, players, pups?
   fleet *forest* *school* *team*

2. Of what are these collections?
   ants *corn* *eggs*
   army, mob, sheaf, bundle, clutch.
   people *rags*

3. Supply the missing word:

   a) a *fleet* of cars
   b) a *staff* of servants
   c) a *host* of angels
   d) a *bunch* of grapes
   e) a *troop* of monkeys

   f) a *shoal* of herring
   g) a *herd* of cattle
   h) a *board* of directors
   i) a *brood* of chickens
   j) a *library* of books

4. Insert the most suitable word in each of the following:

   a) a litter of *cubs*
   b) a band of *musicians*
   c) a building of *rooks*
   d) a plague of *insects*
   e) a bouquet of *flowers*

   f) a cluster of *stars*
   g) a stack of *hay*
   h) a skein of *silk*
   i) a crew of *sailors*
   j) an army of *ants*

5. Give one word for a number of people:

   a) at a concert; *audience*
   b) in church; *congregation*
   c) in the street; *throng*

   d) in a riot; *mob*
   e) in a rowdy scene; *rabble*
   f) at a football match. *crowd*

6. The following words represent a definite number:

   single, couple, brace, pair, dozen.

   Place the words in the phrases best suited to their use:

   a) a *clutch* eggs
   b) a *group* of chairs
   c) a *covey* of grouse

   d) a *pair* of boots
   e) a *single* ticket

7. At my uncle's farm I saw:

   a) a *flock* of sheep
   b) a *litter* of pups
   c) a *swarm* of·bees

   d) a *herd* of cattle
   e) a *brood* of chickens
   f) a *gaggle* of geese

Exercises on Group Terms or Collections continued

8. **Insert the most suitable words in the following sentences:**
   a) He was greeted at the station by a _group_ of friends.
   b) A _gang_ of thieves had broken into the premises.
   c) The old shepherd carefully counted his _flock_ of sheep.
   d) An _army_ of ants moved slowly across our path.
   e) The fishermen saw signs of the presence of a _shoal_ of herring.
   f) At the evening service, the minister preached to a large _congreation_
   g) The attackers were met by a _hail_ of bullets.
   h) His whole _herd_ of cattle had been affected by the drought.
   i) The travellers were hotly pursued by a _pack_ of wolves.
   j) He attended a meeting of the _board_ of directors.

9. The following definitions represent **numeral** words; for example, an aeroplane with *one* set of wings is called a **monoplane**.

   How many can you recognise and properly name?
   a) one person singing _singer_
   b) a single eye-glass _glass eye_
   c) a fabled animal with one horn _rhino_
   d) a two-wheeled cycle _bicycle_
   e) a two-footed animal _human_
   f) an aeroplane with two sets of wings _aeroplane_
   g) a piece of music written for two performers _duet_
   h) two babies born at the same time _twins_
   i) a combat between two people _fight_
   j) a three-legged stand or support _tripod_
   k) three persons singing together _trio_
   l) a three-wheeled cycle _tricycle_
   m) a four-footed animal _sheep_
   n) four persons singing together _quartet_
   o) a period of ten years _decade_
   p) a period of a hundred years _century_
   q) a person aged one hundred years _centenarian_
   r) a Roman commander of one hundred men _centurion_
   s) creatures said to have one hundred feet _centipede_

Similes

Similes compare things which are alike in some respect, although they may be different in their general nature.

1. **Similes showing distinctive qualities of creatures:**

as agile as a monkey	as meek as a lamb
as blind as a bat	as obstinate as a mule
as brave as a lion	as old as Methuselah
as bright as a lark	as patient as Job
as busy as an ant	as playful as a kitten
as busy as a bee	as playful as a puppy
as calm as a cat	as pleased as Punch
as crafty as a fox	as plump as a partridge
as cunning as a fox	as poor as a church mouse
as devoted as a mother	as proud as a peacock
as fast as a deer	as quiet as a mouse
as fast as a hare	as red as a turkey-cock
as fat as a pig	as sick as a dog
as feeble as a child	as silly as a sheep
as fierce as a lion	as slippery as an eel
as flat as a flounder	as slow as a snail
as fleet as a gazelle	as slow as a tortoise
as frisky as a lamb	as sober as a judge
as frisky as a two-year-old	as stolid as a cow
as gentle as a dove	as strong as a horse
as gentle as a lamb	as strong as an ox
as graceful as a swan	as sure-footed as a goat
as hairy as a gorilla	as swift as a deer
as happy as a king	as swift as a hare
as happy as a lark	as swift as a hawk
as happy as a sandboy	as tall as a giant
as harmless as a dove	as tenacious as a bulldog
as heavy as an elephant	as tender as a chicken
as hungry as a hunter	as tender as a shepherd
as hungry as a wolf	as thick as thieves
as industrious as a beaver	as timid as a mouse
as like as two herring	as timid as a rabbit
as loyal as an apostle	as wise as an owl
as mad as a hatter	as wise as Solomon
as mad as a March hare	as white as a ghost

2. **Similes showing special qualities of things:**

as black as coal	as neat as a new pin
as black as soot	as old as the hills
as bold as brass	as open as day
as bright as a button	as pale as death
as brittle as glass	as plain as a pikestaff
as brown as a berry	as purple as the heather
as changeable as the weather	as quick as lightning
as clean as a whistle	as regular as the clock
as clear as a bell	as right as rain
as clear as crystal	as round as a barrel
as cold as charity	as round as an orange
as cold as ice	as safe as houses
as cool as a cucumber	as sharp as a needle
as dead as a doornail	as sharp as a razor
as deaf as a doorpost	as silent as the grave
as drunk as a lord	as smooth as glass
as dry as a bone	as smooth as velvet
as dull as dishwater	as soft as butter
as easy as ABC	as soft as down
as easy as winking	as soft as putty
as fat as butter	as sound as a bell
as fit as a fiddle	as sour as vinegar
as flat as a pancake	as steady as a rock
as fresh as a daisy	as stiff as a poker
as fresh as paint	as straight as an arrow
as good as gold	as straight as a ramrod
as green as grass	as sturdy as an oak
as hard as iron	as sweet as honey
as hard as nails	as thin as a rake
as heavy as lead	as tough as leather
as hot as a furnace	as ugly as sin
as keen as mustard	as warm as wool
as large as life	as weak as water
as light as a feather	as white as a sheet
as alike as two peas	as white as snow

Exercises on Similes

1. We say "as black as coal". Supply the missing words in the following:

   a) as sharp as _needle_   f) as slippery as _an eel_
   b) as keen as _mustard_   g) as swift as _hare_
   c) as brave as _lion_   h) as clear as _crystal_
   d) as sweet as _honey_   i) as light as _a feather_
   e) as cold as _ice_

2. Complete the following:

   a) as _agile_ as a monkey   f) as _steady_ as a rock
   b) as _flat_ as a flounder   g) as _hard_ as iron
   c) as _pleased_ as Punch   h) as _neat_ as a new pin
   d) as _tender_ as a chicken   i) as _timid_ as a rabbit
   e) as _busy_ as a bee   j) as _old_ as the hills

3. Complete the following sentences with suitable words:
   a) The coward was trembling like a _rabbit_ .
   b) His hands were as cold as _ice_ .
   c) The man could swim like a _deer_ .
   d) The baby was as good as _gold_ .
   e) The boy ran like the _wind_ .

4. Pick out (by underlining) the best simile in the following:

   Example: As dry as (a tree, an egg, <u>a bone</u>, an apple).
   a) As flat as (a kettle, <u>a pancake</u>, a loaf, a saucer).
   b) As steady as (<u>a rock</u>, a book, a box, a table).
   c) As fast as (a child, a tortoise, a herring, <u>a deer</u>).
   d) As proud as (a lamb, a daisy, <u>a peacock</u>, a rabbit).
   e) As happy as (a giraffe, <u>a lark</u>, a lobster, a serpent).

5. Add what you consider the most suitable word:
   a) The lake shone like a _diamond_.
   b) The smooth sea was like _glass_ .
   c) The water was as clear as _crystal_ .
   d) The boy climbed the tree like a _monkey_.
   e) His terrified companion stuck to him like a _limpet_ .

Occupations

Describe in a sentence the occupations of the following:

artist	conductor	journalist	postman/woman
athlete	confectioner	judge	reporter
barber	decorator	lawyer	sailor
blacksmith	dentist	locksmith	sculptor
butcher	detective	magistrate	secretary
cabinet-maker	doctor	mason	shepherd
caddie	engineer	matron	shopkeeper
caretaker	explorer	mechanic	soldier
carpenter	farmer	miner	stationer
cashier	florist	minister	steeplejack
chauffeur	gamekeeper	newsagent	surgeon
chemist	glazier	nurse	tailor
cleaner	greengrocer	optician	teacher
clown	grocer	physician	
coastguard	hairdresser	pilot	
cobbler	ironmonger	plumber	
computer programmer	jockey	police officer	
	joiner	porter	

With whom do you associate the following?

anvil	handcuffs	razor	spectacles
awl	harness	rifle	telescope
barrow	knife	roofs	ticket-punch
baton	lancet	safety lamp	tins
briefcase	mail	saw	tractor
cleaver	palette	scales	trumpet
forceps	plane	sheep	ward
furnace	plough	shovel	wig
glasscutter	prescription	solder	
gun	pulpit	spanner	

Name the chief persons connected with the following:

army	hospital	Police Station	school
church	navy	Post Office	ship
college	newspaper	prison	Sunday School
committee	orchestra	railway station	team of players
court of law	Parliament	Salvation Army	workshop

Exercises   on Occupations

1. **What am I called?**
   a) I build stone houses. *mason* ~~porter~~
   b) I carry bags at the railway station. *porter*
   c) I write stories for newspapers. *reporter*
   d) I ride horses in races. *jockey*
   e) I prepare and sell meat. *butcher*

2. **Many shopkeepers draw attention to their places of business by hanging special signs above their shopdoors. What special sign is displayed by**
   a) a bootmaker; *boot*   d) a hairdresser; *scissors*   g) a pawnbroker; *three balls*
   b) a chemist; *prescription*   e) a locksmith; *key*   h) a saddler; *horse*
   c) a fishmonger; *fish*   f) an optician; *glasses*   i) a watchmaker? *watch*

3. **In each of the following give one word for a person who**
   a) attends to people's teeth; *dentist*   g) looks after people's eyes; *optician*
   b) carves in stone; *sculptor*   h) cares for patients in hospital; *doctor*
   c) searches for new lands; *explorer*   i) repairs boots and shoes; *cobbler*
   d) draws plans for buildings; *architect*   j) sells from door to door; *peddlar*
   e) flies an aeroplane; *pilot*   k) studies the stars; *astronomer*
   f) investigates crime; *detective*   l) conducts sales by bidding. *auctioneer*

4. **Arrange the following as you see them advertised in shop windows:**
   chocolate   tomatoes   oranges
   best assorted, good fresh, fine ripe, splendid cooking, sweet juicy, *onions* young spring. *herring*   *apples*

   apples, chocolates, herring, onions, oranges, tomatoes.

Places

Worship

abbey, cathedral, chapel, church, convent, gurdwara, kirk, mandir, monastery, mosque, pagoda, priory, synagogue, tabernacle, temple.

Business

What are the places called where the following are made?

beer, bread, films, flour, iron goods, leather, money, paper, ships, whisky.

Name particular places where the following are sold:

bread, clothes, fish, flowers, fruit, general foodstuffs, meat, milk, newspapers, poultry, spectacles, sweets and chocolates, tobacco, vegetables, writing materials.

Sport

Give particular names of the places where the following are played:

badminton, bowls, boxing, cricket, croquet, football, golf, hockey, putting, rugby, running, skating, sleighing, tennis, wrestling.

General

Give the particular names of the places connected with the following:

Where	Where
aeroplanes are kept	historical relics are shown
bees are kept	law is meted out
birds are kept	operations are performed
bull-fighting is held	orphans are kept
cars are kept	people are buried
chickens are hatched	people lunch for payment
cooks prepare food	plays are shown
criminals are kept	pupils are educated
doctors receive their patients	rooks build their nests
films are shown	soldiers are stationed
fish are kept	water is stored
fruit trees grow	wild animals are kept
gas is stored	young plants and flowers are
grain is stored	reared
grapes are grown	young trees are grown

Receptacles

It is interesting to note the types of containers used to hold and carry foodstuffs, e.g.

bag – cocoa, coffee, rice, sago, sugar;
barrel – apples, beer, oil;
box – apples, butter, currants, fish;
chest – tea, cloves;
sack – flour, potatoes.

Exercises on Receptacles

1. Name the contents you would expect to find in the following:

barrel *apples*	case *clothes*	jug *milk*	sheath *knife*
basin *water*	cask *wine*	keg *beer*	still *whisky*
basket *fruit*	cellar *bottles*	kettle *water*	tank *water*
bath *water*	compact *face powder*	kitbag *uniform*	tankard *beer*
bin *rubbish*	cup *tea*	library *books*	teapot *tea*
boiler *water*	cupboard *crockery*	packet *food*	Thermos (vacuum)
bottle *milk*	decanter *wine*	pan *food cooking*	flask *drink*
bowl *fruit*	drum *oil*	pitcher *water*	till *money*
box *tools*	envelope *letter*	pocket-book *bank notes*	trunk *clothes*
briefcase *documents*	flagon *cider*	portfolio *papers*	tub *water*
butt *wine*	flask *tea*	pot *food cooking*	tumbler *water*
caddy *tea*	gasometer *gas*	punnet *strawberry*	urn *tea*
can *fruit*	goblet *wine*	purse *money*	vase *flowers*
canister *tea*	hamper *food*	safe *money*	vat *liquids*
carafe *wine*	handbag *keys*	satchel *school books*	wallet *money*
carton *juice*	jar *jam*	scabbard *sword*	wardrobe *clothes*

2. In what receptacles or containers would you expect to find the following?

Example: tea – caddy.

money *purse*	jam *jar*	sword *scabbard*
water *reservoir*	coal *scuttle*	flowers *vase*
sauce *bottle*	letter *envelope*	wine *cask*

25

Sounds and Motions

All creatures make sounds and move in a fashion peculiar to their species. Their outstanding characteristics are described by the common adjectives.

Creature	Sound	Motion	Common Adjective
ape	gibbers	swings	ungainly
ass	brays	jogs	stupid
bear	growls	lumbers	clumsy
bee	hums	flits	busy
beetle	drones	crawls	horrid
bull	bellows	charges	angry
cat	purrs	steals	sleek
cow	lows	wanders	stolid
deer	bells	bounds	fallow
dog	barks	runs	faithful
donkey	brays	trots	obstinate
elephant	trumpets	ambles	ponderous
frog	croaks	leaps	clammy
horse	neighs	gallops	noble
hound	bays	bounds	gallant
hyena	screams	prowls	cunning
lamb	bleats	frisks	gentle
lion	roars	prowls	tawny
monkey	chatters	climbs	agile
mouse	squeaks	scampers	timid
person	talks	walks	average
pig	grunts	trots	fat
rabbit	squeals	leaps	timid
serpent	hisses	glides	loathsome
wolf	howls	lopes	lean
bird	whistles	flies	swift
cock	crows	struts	proud
crow	caws	flaps	black
curlew	pipes	flits	lonely
duck	quacks	waddles	waddling
eagle	screams	swoops	proud
hen	cackles	struts	domestic
lark	sings	soars	gentle
owl	hoots	flits	tawny

Creature	Sound	Motion	Common Adjective
parrot	screeches	flits	saucy
pigeon	coos	flutters	gentle
robin	chirps	hops	little
seagull	screams	glides	tireless
sparrow	chirps	flits	little
swallow	twitters	dives	swift
turkey	gobbles	struts	plump
wren	warbles	hops	tiny

aquiline	– like an eagle	ferine	– like a wild beast
asinine	– like an ass	leonine	– like a lion
bovine	– like a cow or ox	lupine	– like a wolf
canine	– like a dog	ovine	– like a sheep
corvine	– like a crow	piscine	– like a fish
elephantine	– like an elephant	porcine	– like a pig
equine	– like a horse	tigrine	– like a tiger
feline	– like a cat	vulpine	– like a fox

Certain words are used in **imitation** of the sounds made by creatures, e.g.

ass	– hee-haw	**duck**	– quack
cat	– me-ow	**hen**	– cluck
cock	– cock-a-doodle-do	**owl**	– tu-whoo
cow	– moo	**rook**	– caw
cuckoo	– cuckoo	**sheep**	– baa
dog	– woof	**sparrow**	– tweet-tweet

The following verbs are obtained from the **habits** of creatures:

to ape	– to imitate foolishly
to badger	– to worry or tease
to crow	– to boast or swagger
to dog	– to follow or track
to duck	– to dip or plunge
to ferret	– to search out
to fox	– to act cunningly
to hound	– to pursue relentlessly
to ram	– to drive or push into
to wolf	– to eat greedily

Exercises | on Sounds and Motions

1. Animals make different sounds, e.g. The dog **barks**.

   What sounds are made by the following animals?
   donkey, elephant, horse, pig, wolf, monkey, deer, cow, bear, hyena.

   brays trumpets neighs grunts howls chatters bells moo growl screams

2. Write the names of the creatures:

   The _hound_ bays.   The _frog_ croaks.
   The _serpent_ hisses.   The _cat_ purrs.
   The _cock_ crows.   The _turkey_ gobbles.
   The _sheep_ bleats.   The _lion_ roars.
   The _crow_ caws.   The _duck_ quacks.

3. Describe the movements of the following, e.g. The horse **gallops**.

   The frog _leaps_   The duck _waddles_
   The monkey _climbs_   The lamb _frisks_
   The wolf _lopes_   The lark _soars_
   The seagull _glides_   The bear _lumbers_

4. Apply the most fitting adjective:

   sleek, cunning, obstinate, fat, tireless, loathsome, gentle, faithful.

   The _obstinate_ mule.   The _cunning_ fox.
   The _fat_ pig.   The _gentle_ lamb.
   The _faithful_ dog.   The _sleek_ cat.
   The _loathsome_ serpent.   The _tireless_ seagull.

5. What is meant by calling a person

   a) an ape _foolish_   h) a fox _cunningly_   o) a rabbit _timid_
   b) an ass _asinine_   i) a goat _nimble_   p) a sheep _ovine_
   c) a bear _clumsy_   j) a horse _noble_   q) a snail _slow_
   d) a bull _angry_   k) a hound _gallant_   r) a swine _coarse_
   e) a dog _faithful_   l) a lamb _gentle_   s) a tortoise _slow_
   f) a donkey _stupid_   m) a lion _leonine_   t) a viper _scary_
   g) an elephant _elephantine_ n) a pig _porcine_   u) a wolf? _leer_

Exercises on Sounds and Motions continued

6. **Which creatures were the speakers thinking of when they said?**
   a) "The man bellowed with rage." *bull*
   b) "He has the hump today." *camel*
   c) "We were stung by his remarks." *bee*
   d) "Don't crow so loudly." *cock*
   e) "The officer barked an order." *dog*
   f) "The witch spoke in a croaky voice." *frog*
   g) "He grunted in reply." *pig*
   h) "The girls were chattering in the hall." *monkey*
   i) "Why are you galloping along the corridor?" *horse*
   j) "The boy howled when he was caught." *wolf*
   k) "The wicked old woman cackled loudly as she stirred the pot." *hen*
   l) "The lecturer's voice droned on and on." *bee*
   m) "The little girl screeched with delight." *parrot*
   n) "The captain snorted in disgust." *horse*
   o) "The curious child prowled about the room." *hyena*
   p) "Loud hooting interrupted the speech." *owl*

7. **Explain the words underlined in the following sentences:**
   a) He had an <u>aquiline</u> nose. *like an eagle*
   b) The burglar walked with a <u>feline</u> tread. *like a cat*
   c) The yokel had a <u>bovine</u> look. *like a cow*
   d) He was scolded for his <u>asinine</u> conduct. *like an ass*
   e) They had the appearance of sharp <u>canine</u> teeth. *like a dog*

8. **What feeling is expressed by**
   a) a chuckle *amusement*   e) a hoot *derision*   i) a sigh *disappointed*
   b) a groan *pain*   f) a howl *pain*   j) a sniff *snob*
   c) a growl *angry*   g) a roar *angry*   k) a snort *contempt*
   d) a grunt *undecided*   h) a screech *pain*   l) a squeal? *timidity*

9. **Complete the following:**

   On a recent visit to a large farm I heard various animal sounds. I heard

   a cock *crowing*   cows *lowing*
   pigs *grunting*   ducks *quacking*
   horses *neighing*   lambs *bleating*
   turkeys *gobbling*   and a dog *barking*

Sounds made by Objects

Note that the words have been formed to resemble the sounds made by the objects.

babble of a stream	ping of a bullet
bang of a door	popping of corks
beat of a drum	purr of an engine
blare of a trumpet	rattling of dishes
blast of an explosion	report of a rifle
booming of a gun	ring of metal
bubbling of water	ring of a telephone
buzz of a saw	ringing of bells
call of a bugle	roar of a torrent
chime of a bell (large)	rumble of a train
chime of a clock	rustle of silk
chug of an engine	rustling of leaves
clang of an anvil	scrape of a bow
clang of a bell	screeching of brakes
clanking of chains	shriek of a whistle
clatter of hoofs	shuffling of feet
clink of a coin	sighing of the wind
crack of a whip	singing of the kettle
crackling of wood	skirl of the bagpipes
creak of a hinge	slam of a door
crinkle of paper	splutter of an engine
dripping of water	swish of skirts
grinding of brakes	throb of an engine
gurgle of a stream	thunder of hoofs
hissing of steam	tick of a clock
hoot of a horn	tinkle of a bell (small)
howling of the wind	tinkle of glass
jangling of chains	toot of a horn
jingle of coins	tramp of feet
lapping of water	twang of a bow
lash of a whip	wail of a siren
murmur of a stream	whack of a cane
patter of feet	whirring of wings
patter of rain	whoosh of a rocket
pealing of bells	

Exercises on Sounds made by Objects

1. Insert suitable words in the blank spaces.

   Example: The **beat** of a drum.
   The _creak_ of a hinge.   The _crack_ of a whip.
   The _grinding_ of brakes.   The _hissing_ of steam.
   The _patter_ of feet.   The _rustle_ of silk.
   The _call_ of a bugle.   The _tick_ of a clock.

2. Supply the missing words.

   Example: The clatter of **hoofs**.
   The pealing of _bells_   The popping of _corks_
   The booming of _a gun_   The skirl of the _~~the~~ bagpipes_
   The crinkle of _paper_   The throb of an _engine_
   The slam of a _door_   The toot of a _horn_

3. Use the right words in the following:
   A boiling kettle _singing_.
   Frying fat _sizzles_ in the pan.
   Coins _clink_ in the bag.
   The heavy bar fell with a _thud_.
   Suddenly we heard the _thunder_ of hoofs.
   We were awakened by the _chime_ of the big church clock.
   The passengers heard the loud _grinding_ of brakes.
   The rude boy _slammed_ the door behind him.
   The north wind _howling_ in the chimney.
   I heard the _report_ of a rifle.
   The rain _pattered_ on the window.
   Thunder _rumbled_.

4. Complete the following by adding a sentence which indicates the cause of the sound. The first is done for you:
   a) Toot! Toot! The sound of a car horn warned us of danger.
   b) Bang! The sound of a gunshot that warned us of the riot
   c) Boom! The sound of a bomb exploding warned us to go to anywhere and get delayed
   d) Crash! The sound of a car crash told us that we would be
   e) Plop! The sound of the last potato boiling told us that dinner was ready
   f) Rat-tat-tat! The sound of the spoon told us that Michael was playing
   g) Splash! The sound of Amy jumping into the pool told us that we had to go save her
   h) Tick-tock! The sound of the clock told us to go to bed
   i) Ting-a-ling! The sound of the bell told us that food was ready

Classification

All things on earth may be divided into two classes:

◆ **Animate** (living things).

◆ **Inanimate** (things having no life).

1. **The animate or living things** consist of creatures and plants. Creatures can eat, grow and move about from place to place, e.g. animals including people, birds, fishes, insects, reptiles. Plants are fixed by means of roots and although they can absorb food and grow they cannot move about from place to place, e.g. trees, flowers, vegetables.

2. **The inanimate or things having no life** are fixed, cannot eat, cannot grow and cannot move about from place to place, e.g. stone, cloth, knife.

Every object can be placed in a certain general class either because of its resemblance to other things or because of its purpose or use. **The following are general classes:** animals, birds, insects, fishes, reptiles, flowers, fruits, trees, vegetables, minerals, liquids, apparel, occupations, places, utensils, ships, games, vehicles, cereals, coins, instruments.

Exercises on Classification

1. Write one name for each of the following groups, e.g.
   iron, lead, copper: **metals**
   a) lion, bear, goat, mouse __animals__
   b) jacket, blouse, trousers, skirt __clothes__
   c) canary, eagle, pigeon, magpie __birds__
   d) lawyer, butcher, engineer, doctor __occupation__
   e) beetle, ant, bee, locust __insects__
   f) bus, car, lorry, wagon __vehicles__
   g) daffodil, tulip, violet, crocus __flowers__
   h) cup, saucer, bowl, plate __crockery__
   i) flounder, haddock, trout, herring __fish__
   j) autumn, winter, spring, summer __seasons__
   j) shoes, Wellingtons, boots, slippers __footwear__
   l) potato, carrot, beetroot, turnip __vegetables__
   m) hawthorn, palm, beech, chestnut __trees__
   n) bread, butter, meat, porridge __food__
   o) mango, orange, banana, lemon __fruit__
   p) water, milk, brine, paraffin __liquids__
   q) wheat, maize, oats, barley __grains or__
   r) aunt, uncle, niece, cousin __relatives__
   s) twelve, seven, twenty, eight __numbers__
   t) football, hockey, rugby, cricket __ball games__

32

Exercises   on Classification continued

2. In the following lists of words, one word seems out of place. Underline the word you consider is not in the same class. The first is done for you.

   (1)   rose, hibiscus, poinsettia, <u>tomato</u>, carnation
   (2)   hen, <u>hare</u>, duck, goose, turkey
   (3)   pine, oak, <u>violet</u>, rhododendron, ash
   (4)   <u>slate</u>, gold, silver, iron, lead
   (5)   potato, <u>lemon</u>, maize, cauliflower, spinach
   (6)   granite, <u>cement</u>, limestone, marble, whinstone
   (7)   oats, wheat, <u>loaf</u>, sugarcane, barley
   (8)   salmon, <u>whale</u>, snapper, trout, mullet
   (9)   diamond, emerald, <u>pearl</u>, ruby, sapphire
   (10) <u>Mumbai</u>, London, Washington, Islamabad, Kingston
   (11) Ireland, Sri Lanka, Jamaica, Cyprus, <u>Mexico</u>
   (12) tea, coffee, cocoa, chocolate, <u>biscuit</u>
   (13) rain, sleet, snow, <u>heat</u>, hail
   (14) bacon, <u>milk</u>, cheese, butter, bread
   (15) <u>shield</u>, lance, dagger, gun, spear
   (16) bus, tractor, <u>yacht</u>, train, lorry
   (17) cottage, mansion, palace, bungalow, <u>warehouse</u>
   (18) <u>tomatoes</u>, journeys, excursions, voyages, trips
   (19) birch, <u>maize</u>, maple, chestnut, pine
   (20) man, boy, master, <u>princess</u>, uncle
   (21) rose, <u>palm</u>, orchid, lily, primrose
   (22) Marcus, <u>Maria</u>, Martin, Mohammed, Melvyn
   (23) <u>cupboard</u>, kitchen, bathroom, bedroom, hall
   (24) orange, <u>potato</u>, cherry, apple, banana
   (25) beer, milk, <u>cotton</u>, wine, water
   (26) boy, <u>wagon</u>, kitten, girl, puppy
   (27) plate, cup, saucer, bowl, <s>fork</s>
   (28) <u>radiator</u>, saxophone, trumpet, piano, guitar
   (29) Pakistan, Spain, <u>Delhi</u>, Brazil, Malaysia
   (30) elephant, tiger, giraffe, <s>crocodile</s>, horse
   (31) salt, sauce, <s>plate</s>, mustard, pepper
   (32) spinster, lady, niece, <u>uncle</u>, sister
   (33) chair, <u>carpet</u>, wardrobe, stool, table
   (34) baker, butcher, fisherman, <s>barber</s>, cook
   (35) pigeon, parrot, <u>penguin</u>, sparrow, swallow
   (36) basket, purse, <u>kettle</u>, trunk, scabbard

Exercises on Classification continued

3. Put a line under one of the same kind as the first three in each line. The first is done for you.

(1)	cap, balmoral, hat	face, book, <u>turban</u>, coat, hatchet
(2)	jug, teapot, cup	<u>bowl</u>, loaf, hammer, key, door
(3)	stork, hen, eagle	egg, butterfly, <u>owl</u>, nest, mouse
(4)	tulip, daisy, violet	foot, cup, brush, <u>rose</u>, scissors
(5)	eye, nose, mouth	hand, leg, knee, arm, <u>ear</u>
(6)	tin, copper, zinc	basin, <u>iron</u>, marble, corn, carrot
(7)	tuna, swordfish, mackerel	gate, street, orange, ship, <u>trout</u>
(8)	chair, table, stool	<u>sofa</u>, pot, door, car, tub
(9)	buffalo, monkey, rat	wasp, parrot, <u>lion</u>, canary
(10)	apple, banana, plum	<u>peach</u>, violet, onion, hawthorn
(11)	iron, lead, copper	marble, coal, slate, <u>zinc</u>
(12)	ant, mosquito, moth	rabbit, <u>fly</u>, dog, snake
(13)	Nairobi, London, Kingston	Trinidad, Scotland, Kenya, <u>Abuja</u>
(14)	steamer, yacht, submarine	aeroplane, <u>trawler</u>, motor, train
(15)	caramel, cake, ice-cream	book, pencil, <u>toffee</u>, ruler
(16)	flamingo, buzzard, kite	grasshopper, fox, <u>penguin</u>, seal
(17)	frock, jacket, coat	<u>blouse</u>, curtain, sheet, carpet
(18)	car, train, taxi	bicycle, steamer, canoe, seaplane
(19)	tuna, salmon, snapper	vulture, <u>barracuda</u>, snail, cat
(20)	tennis, hockey, golf	darts, <u>volleyball</u>, boxing, whist
(21)	tulip, geranium, lily	paw-paw, potato, <u>rose</u>, diamond
(22)	cocoa, coffee, water	bread, <u>soup</u>, pepper, sugar
(23)	violin, piano, harp	drum, bugle, <u>guitar</u>, trombone
(24)	cabbage, carrot, potato	lilac, <u>yam</u>, pine, turkey
(25)	barber, florist, tailor	miner, driver, cameraman, <u>shoemaker</u>
(26)	ankle, foot, knee	head, wrist, <u>thigh</u>, nose
(27)	box, vase, bowl	notebook, window, <u>bin</u>, hoe
(28)	terrier, collie, greyhound	tiger, <u>spaniel</u>, hyena, lion
(29)	sandals, shoes, boots	gloves, trousers, <u>slippers</u>, pockets
(30)	oak, pine, fir	<u>teak</u>, lettuce, poinsettia, shark

Exercises   on Classification continued

4. Underline the word (in brackets) which has a **similar meaning** to the first three words in each line. The first is done for you.

   a) cost, fee, charge   (money, <u>price</u>, purse, silver)
   b) mount, soar, rise   (depart, arrive, retire, <u>ascend</u>)
   c) hail, greet, salute   (alarm, habit, <u>welcome</u>, ignore)
   d) vigilant, alert, wary   (aloft, believe, attempt, <u>watchful</u>)
   e) notice, perceive, behold   (provide, <u>observe</u>, advise, obtain)
   f) concluded, finished, ended   (commenced, allowed, <u>completed</u>, carried)
   g) peace, calm, rest   (<u>quietness</u>, worry, agitated, movement)
   h) support, help, aid   (abandon, remedy, <u>assist</u>, ignore)
   i) walked, tramped, marched   (chuckled, <u>plodded</u>, glanced, knocked)
   j) conquer, defeat, overcome   (bully, retire, <u>vanquish</u>, submit)
   k) edge, border, fringe   (<u>margin</u>, centre, interior, cover)
   l) occupied, diligent, busy   (lazy, helpless, indolent, <u>industrious</u>)
   m) hinder, retard, delay   (progress, <u>obstruct</u>, reveal, select)
   n) vagabond, wanderer, tramp   (milliner, caddie, collector, <u>vagrant</u>)
   o) desert, forsake, leave   (protect, <u>abandon</u>, pursue, arrive)
   p) serious, sober, solemn   (blunt, <u>grave</u>, tired, insulted)
   q) weep, cry, wail   (deafen, bite, <u>whimper</u>, frighten)
   r) pleased, happy, delighted   (friendly, agreeable, kind, <u>cheerful</u>)
   s) stupid, silly, foolish   (stylish, trivial, <u>absurd</u>, helpless)
   t) annoy, pester, torment   (deceive, <u>irritate</u>, influence, hinder)

Gradation

There are five words in each row. You are asked to place them in order of size (smallest first). The first is done for you.

1. boy, baby, man, child, youth

    baby, child, boy, youth, man

2. ten, one, million, thousand, hundred

    one, ten, hundred, thousand, million

3. litre, millilitre, decalitre, decilitre, hectolitre

    millitre, decilitre, litre, decalitre, hectolitre

4. year, millennium, century, month, day

    day, month, year, century, millennium

5. minute, week, second, hour, day

    second, minute, hour, day, week

6. cow, cat, elephant, sheep, mouse

    mouse, cat, sheep, cow, elephant

7. kettle, cup, pail, teapot, tub

    cup, teapot, kettle, pail, tub

8. mansion, hut, bungalow, cottage, palace

    hut, bungalow, cottage, mansion, palace

9. metre, centimetre, kilometre, millimetre

    millimetre, centimetre, metre, kilometre

10. shark, sardine, whale, cod, snapper

    sardine, snapper, cod, shark, whale

11. hen, pigeon, robin, ostrich, turkey

    robin, pigeon, hen, turkey, ostrich

12. city, country, town, continent, village

    village, town, city, country, continent

13. bean, pea, cabbage, onion, turnip

    pea, bean, onion, turnip, cabbage

14. ocean, river, spring, stream, sea

    spring, stream, river, sea, ocean

36

15. banana, paw-paw, orange, cherry, melon

cherry, orange, banana, paw-paw, melon

16. piano, trombone, pipe-organ, violin, flute

flute, violin, trombone, piano, pipe-organ

17. wallet, purse, safe, vault, handbag

purse, wallet, handbag, safe, vault

18. fly, midge, ant, wasp, butterfly

midge, fly, ant, wasp, butterfly

19. sentence, letter, paragraph, word, chapter

letter, word, sentence, paragraph, chapter

Here are some harder examples. Grade each group of five words according to the word in the bracket (least first):

(sound) giggled, laughed, smiled, guffawed, chuckled

smiled, chuckled, giggled, laughed, guffawed

(feeling) punched, touched, battered, tapped, knocked

touched, tapped, knocked, punched, battered

(speed) strode, galloped, trotted, cantered, walked

walked, strode, trotted, cantered, galloped

(sound) shrieked, talked, shouted, whispered, roared

whispered, talked, shouted, shrieked, roared

(feeling) fingered, slapped, patted, caressed, walloped

fingered, patted, caressed, slapped, walloped

(speed) marched, sauntered, strode, walked, shuffled

shuffled, sauntered, walked, strode, marched

(sound) crooned, hummed, lilted, yodelled, sang

hummed, crooned, lilted, sang, yodelled

(time) looked, stared, glimpsed, gazed, glanced

glimpsed, glanced, looked, stared, gazed

Association

Underline the two words in the brackets which are associated with (or part of) the first word in bold type. The first is done for you.

1. **boot** (sleeve, heel, handle, sole, paper)

2. **chair** (saucer, poker, arm, tongs, leg)

3. **bed** (mattress, carpet, ribbon, blanket, blouse)

4. **bath** (book, soap, glove, vase, sponge)

5. **room** (flour, ceiling, drum, floor, vegetable)

6. **tree** (wall, trunk, chalk, bough, lamp)

7. **clock** (hands, wristlet, face, shovel, cushion)

8. **flower** (purse, stem, seat, lard, petals)

9. **bird** (sheet, wings, beak, canoe, factory)

10. **bee** (sting, mirror, bread, honey, banana)

11. **knife** (acorn, blade, opposite, handle, coat)

12. **kettle** (spout, plate, butter, basket, lid)

13. **window** (spoon, glass, pillow, bullet, curtains)

14. **car** (chart, anvil, engine, tyres, grate)

15. **sun** (rays, harbour, sermon, heat, crescent)

16. **bottle** (handle, paper, chimney, neck, cork)

17. **rifle** (barrel, trigger, candle, mirror, arrow)

18. **fork** (cellar, prongs, beggar, handle, blade)

19. **fish** (fodder, arms, gills, mutton, fins)

20. **torch** (bulb, furnace, battery, meter, grate)

21. **door** (model, knob, disease, drawer, hinges)

22. **bicycle** (pedals, hangar, bowl, pump, gangway)

23. **pillow** (rug, slip, cloak, bolster, pinafore)

24. **ship** (hood, melody, bridge, trolley, bow)

25. **aeroplane** (funnel, wings, tail, tunnel, paddle)

26. **horse** (bridle, crystal, branch, mane, horns)

38

27. **fire**	(errand, smoke, boots, comb, flame)
28. **piano**	(buttons, fatigue, keys, pedals, pencil)
29. **potato**	(forest, peelings, bark, gown, chips)
30. **hat**	(crown, glue, pouch, brim, pocket)
31. **vehicle**	(velvet, brakes, wheels, cotton, scissors)
32. **window**	(cords, pane, basin, inventor, easel)
33. **boot**	(knuckle, hatchet, upper, jacket, tongue)
34. **pipe**	(granite, towel, packet, bowl, stem)
35. **tree**	(fork, telegraph, foliage, muslin, cabbage)
36. **fruit**	(marble, core, turnip, rind, salmon)
37. **school**	(horse, teacher, parrot, article, book)
38. **house**	(compartment, gable, cock-pit, scuppers, eaves)
39. **telephone**	(paragraph, scabbard, receiver, needle, booth)
40. **barrel**	(fatigue, staves, square, hoops, spokes)

Here are more examples with particular reference to parts of our body and their actions:

ear	(deafness, cantered, listening, noticed, tumbled)
mouth	(pushed, strode, glancing, tasting, chewing)
nose	(smiled, sniffed, walked, odour, roared)
eye	(sang, lashes, laughed, blinked, swinging)
face	(folded, smile, yodelled, grin, toddled)
head	(muttered, sauntered, ache, flying, nodding)
arms	(trotted, mumbled, folded, waving, chanted)
hands	(writing, strolling, kicking, wink, clasp)
legs	(crooned, crossed, fingered, smiling, running)
feet	(dancing, waving, paddling, shouting, grinning)

Analogies

Put in the suitable words in the spaces below:

Example: Little is to big as dwarf is to giant.

1. Spider is to fly as cat is to _mice_ .

2. Sheep is to mutton as pig is to _pork_ .

3. Steamer is to pier as train is to _platform_ .

4. Boy is to girl as _man_ is to woman.

5. June is to July as _April_ is to May.

6. High is to low as _up_ is to down.

7. North is to _south_ as east is to west.

8. Uncle is to _nephew_ as aunt is to niece.

9. Soldier is to _army_ as sailor is to navy.

10. _Bray_ is to donkey as neigh is to horse.

11. _Finger_ is to hand as toe is to foot.

12. _Feathers_ are to birds as scales are to fish.

13. Tear is to sorrow as smile is to _happiness_ .

14. Wrist is to arm as ankle is to _leg_ .

15. One is to ten as ten is to _hundred_ .

16. Arrow is to bow as _bullet_ is to rifle.

17. Cat is to kitten as _dog_ is to pup.

18. Foot is to man as _hoof_ is to horse.

19. Father is to _son_ as mother is to daughter.

20. Artist is to _picture_ as author is to book.

21. Water is to _ice_ as liquid is to solid.

22. _Swan_ is to cygnet as pig is to piglet.

23. _Shoal_ is to herring as school is to whales.

24. _Bee_ is to hive as cow is to cowshed.

25. Wing is to bird as fin is to _fish_ .

26. Rich is to poor as ancient is to _modern_ .

27. **One** is to **single** as **two** is to ___double___.

28. **Flock** is to **sheep** as ___herd___ is to **cattle**. ✓

29. **Here** is to **there** as ___this___ is to **that**.

30. **Day** is to **week** as ___month___ is to **year**.

31. **Eat** is to ___ateest___ as **go** is to **went**.

32. **Oil** is to ___bottle___ as **tea** is to **caddy**.

33. **Steam** is to ___water___ as **smoke** is to **fire**.

34. ___Pig___ is to **sty** as **horse** is to **stable**.

35. ___Hot___ is to **cold** as **seldom** is to **often**.

36. ___Water___ is to **fish** as **air** is to **bird**.

37. **Table** is to **wood** as **window** is to ___glass___.

38. **Food** is to **hungry** as **drink** is to ___thirsty___.

39. **Statue** is to **sculptor** as **book** is to ___author___.

40. **Wheel** is to **spoke** as **flower** is to ___petlals___.

41. **Nose** is to **smell** as ___mouth/tongue___ is to **taste**.

42. **Wrist** is to **cuff** as ___neck___ is to **collar**.

43. **Walk** is to **legs** as ___fly___ is to **wings**.

44. **Island** is to **sea** as ___lake___ is to **land**.

45. **Knife** is to ___cut___ as **gun** is to **shoot**.

46. **Picture** is to ___wall___ as **carpet** is to **floor**.

47. **Graceful** is to ___clumsy ting___ as **polite** is to **rude**.

48. **Descend** is to ___depth___ as **ascend** is to **height**.

49. ___Water___ is to **pipes** as **electricity** is to **wires**.

50. ___Steeple___ is to **church** as **tower** is to **castle**.

51. ___Tree___ is to **forest** as **sheep** is to **flock**.

52. ___Shell___ is to **egg** as **rind** is to **orange**.

53. **Constable** is to **thief** as **gamekeeper** is to ___poacher___.

54. **Whisper** is to **shout** as **walk** is to ___run___.

55. **Hearing** is to **ear** as **sight** is to ___eye___.

It Makes You Think

1. Here is a list of Christmas presents which arrived at the Browns' house:

   diary, razor, knitting-bag, chocolates, saw, cigarettes, grapes and a fishing-rod.
   a) **Mr Brown** has a beard, likes woodwork, but does not smoke. ✓
   b) **Mrs Brown** is ill in bed, but able to sit up and use her hands. ✓
   c) **John Brown** is twenty years old, clean-shaven, and does not like fishing. ✓
   d) **Mary Brown** is twelve years old, keen on writing, and fond of sweets. ✓

   Distribute the presents on the above list to each member of the family.

2. On one side of my street the homes all have odd numbers, ending with the baker's which is No. 17. On the other side the numbers are all even, ending with the draper's which is No. 18. Fred Thomson is my next-door-neighbour and his house is No. 10. You pass my house when walking from the draper's to Fred's house.

   What number is my house? No. 12. ✓

3. A policeman was on his rounds one night when he saw a man with a box under his arm come out of a house and hurry down the street. Later the constable found that some jewels had been stolen from the house. The officer remembered that the man he had seen wore a long black coat. He had also noticed that the man had a beard and was lame in his right leg. Next day the following four men were detained:

   John Smith – bearded, long black coat, lame in left leg.
   Tom Taylor – bearded, short black coat, lame in right leg.
   Jack Jones – lame in left leg, short black coat, bearded.
   Jim Baker – long black coat, lame in right leg, bearded.

   If you were the policeman, whom would you consider guilty? Jim Baker ✓

4. The sentences below, when properly arranged, form a short story. Indicate their correct order by numbering them from **1** to **5** within the brackets:

(3) The lad was cast ashore on a lonely island near the scene of the tragedy.

(5) After many exciting adventures he returned to England none the worse for his experience.

(1) Robinson Crusoe went to sea when he was nineteen years of age.

(4) Luckily he managed to obtain from the wreck many things which proved useful to him during his stay on the island.

(2) On his first voyage, the ship encountered a terrible storm and foundered on a rock.

5. In a very dark cupboard there is a heap of twenty socks, all of the same size, ten of which are grey and ten blue. **How many socks must you pick up** in order to make sure that you obtain **a pair of the same colour?** *three*

6. My clock has gone wrong and chimes three times at one o'clock, four times at two o'clock, and so on. It is also half-an-hour fast. **What is the correct time when the clock has just chimed eight?** *5.30*

7. Tom is twice as old as Mary, but he is two years younger than Jim. What is Mary's age if Jim will be twenty years old in two years' time? *8*

An Odd Word or Two

Where does a man buy a cap for his knee,
Or a key for a lock of his hair?
Should his eyes be called an academy
Because there are pupils there?

In the crown of his head what gems are found?
Who crosses the bridge of his nose?
Can he use, if a picture requires to be hung,
The nails on the ends of his toes?

If the crook of his elbow is put in gaol,
I'd say, "What did he do?"
But how does he sharpen his shoulder-blades?
I'm hanged if I know. Do you?

Absurdities

Anything which is absurd is utterly foolish and unreasonable. Can you explain what is absurd in the following?

1. I had six pencils altogether and gave away three of them to my little brother. I had nine pencils left. *6-3 =3 not 9*

2. To sweeten his tea the boy put a spoonful of salt in it. *Salt = sour Sugar, sweet*

3. The man is not so tall as he was when a baby. *You grow taller as you get older*

4. The express train sped along swiftly and silently as it had square wheels. *If it had square wheels it would not move*

5. I hope to attend the concert which took place last week. *If it took place last week you can't attend it.*

6. The witness was asked, "Were you near the horse when it kicked you?" *If it kicked you then you have to be near it*

7. A tramp, wishing to lengthen his blanket, took a bit off the top and added it to the bottom. *He is just making no difference*

8. "Kind sir! Please give me a copper as I am deaf and dumb," cried the old beggar.

9. "Keep moving, please! If everybody was to stand there, how would the rest of the people manage to get past?"

10. The storm, which began yesterday, has continued for three days without a break. *If it started yesterday it*

11. "The elephant is a bonnie bird,
    It flits from bough to bough,
    It makes its nest in the rhubarb tree,
    And whistles like a cow."
    A elephant can't fly

12. "'Twas in the month of Liverpool,
    In the city of July,
    The rain was snowing heavily,
    And the streets were very dry."
    There is no month of Liverpool

13. Two Inuit were having a chat. The weather was so cold that, when one of them spoke, his words froze into blocks of ice. The other had to melt the blocks on a frying pan in order to find out what his friend had been saying to him. *words do not freeze*

14. One day at the seaside a man dived from a high platform. When he was half-way down he suddenly noticed that the tide was out and that he would strike his head on the rocks below. This frightened him so much that he changed his mind and jumped back to the platform. *you can't jump back up.*

15. A father wrote to his son, "I enclose a postal order. If you do not receive this letter, please let me know at once." *If he dosen't receive it he won't know about it.*

16. A magician was showing his favourite trick. From the roof of the stage hung a long rope, at the end of which was a hook. An assistant entered and placed a pail of water on the hook. Waving his hands and shouting some strange words, the conjurer covered the pail of water with a magic cloth. A few seconds later he snatched the cloth away and, lo and behold! the pail had disappeared and the water was left hanging on the hook. *water is a liquid it would just fall*

17. It is much safer to travel in a car than in a train, because in a train accident hundreds of people may be injured, while in a car accident there are never more than a few people injured.

18. The proud owner said to his friend, "This clock is so old that the moving shadow of the pendulum has worn away the wood at the back." *If he was proud he would be saying good things about it*

19. In some countries it is against the law for a man to marry his widow's sister. *His not dead so his wife is not a widow.*

20. Old John Smith lived in a small cottage, which stood on the top of a barren hill and faced the east. From the foot of the hill a grassy plain stretched in every direction as far as the eye could see. On the evening of John's thirtieth birthday, while he was sitting on the front door-step, watching the setting sun, he noticed a horseman riding down to the cottage. The trees made it difficult for him to see clearly, but he perceived that the horseman had only one arm. When, however, he got a closer view, he recognised the visitor as his son James, who had left home some twenty years before. On seeing his father, James immediately dismounted, ran towards him, and threw his arms round his neck. *He only has one arm so he threw a arm around him.*

Abbreviations

An abbreviation is the shortening of a word to fewer letters. These letters are used in place of a word for brevity. It used to be customary to mark abbreviations with a full stop, but now it is quite correct to omit them. In some cases using the stop helps to avoid confusion, e.g. A.1.

Abbreviation	Word in Full	Meaning
@	at	
AA	Automobile Association	
AD	*Anno Domini*	In the year of our Lord
AIDS	Acquired Immune Deficiency Syndrome	
a.m.	*ante meridiem*	Before noon
A.1		First class (of ships)
BA	Bachelor of Arts	
BBC	British Broadcasting Corporation	
BC	Before Christ	
BD	Bachelor of Divinity	
BL	Bachelor of Law	
BMA	British Medical Association	
BSc	Bachelor of Science	
C	centigrade or Celsius	
CA	Chartered Accountant	
ChB	Bachelor of Surgery	
CIA	Central Intelligence Agency	
CID	Criminal Investigation Department	
CNN	Cable News Network	
Co.	Company or County	
c.o.d.	cash on delivery	
DIY	do-it-yourself	
do	ditto	
Dr	Doctor	
DV	Deo volente	God willing
e.g.	*exempli gratia*	for example
ER	Elizabeth Regina	Queen Elizabeth II
Esq.	Esquire	
etc.	*et cetera*	and the rest
EU	European Union	
F	Fahrenheit	
ff	following	
FIFA	International Football Federation	

Abbreviation	Word in Full	Meaning
GCSE	General Certificate of Secondary Education	
GDP	gross domestic product	
GMT	Greenwich Mean Time	
HE	His or Her Excellency	
HH	His Holiness	
HM	His or Her Majesty	
HMS	His or Her Majesty's Ship or Service	
hp	horse-power	
HRH	His or Her Royal Highness	
IDD	International Direct Dialling	
i.e.	*id est*	that is
IMF	International Monetary Fund	
inst.	instant	this month
IOU	I owe you	
JP	Justice of the Peace	
km	kilometre	
LA	Los Angeles	
lat.	latitude	
lbw	leg before wicket	
LLB	Bachelor of Laws	
Ltd	Limited	
MA	Master of Arts	
MBA	Master of Business Administration	
MP	Member of Parliament	
mph	miles per hour	
Mr	Mister	
Mrs	Mistress	
Ms		title for a woman (neither Miss nor Mrs)
NASA	National Aeronautics and Space Administration	
NATO	North Atlantic Treaty Organisation	
nb	*nota bene*	note well, take note
No	numero	number
NYC	New York City	
OHMS	On His or Her Majesty's Service	
OK		all correct
OXFAM	Oxford Committee for Famine Relief	

47

Abbreviation	Word in Full	Meaning
PAYE	Pay as You Earn	
per cent	*per centum*	in each hundred
PIA	Pakistan International Airlines	
PM	Prime Minister	
p.m.	*post meridiem*	after noon
PO	Post Office	
pp	pages	
Pres.	President	
PS	*post scriptum*	written after
PTO	Please turn over	
RAC	Royal Automobile Club	
RAF	Royal Air Force	
RAM	Random Access Memory	
RC	Roman Catholic	
RIP	*Requiescat in pace*	may he or she rest in peace
RN	Royal Navy	
ROM	read-only memory	
RSVP	*répondez, s'il vous plaît*	reply, if you please
SA	Salvation Army	
SS	Steam-ship or Sailing-ship	
TA	Territorial Army	
TUC	Trades Union Congress	
UK	United Kingdom	
ult.	*ultimo*	last month
UN	United Nations	
UNESCO	United Nations Educational, Scientific and Cultural Organisation	
UNICEF	United Nations International Children's Emergency Fund	
USA	United States of America	
v.	*versus*	against
VAT	Value Added Tax	
viz.	*videlicet*	namely
WP	word processing / processor	
www	world wide web	
YMCA	Young Men's Christian Association	
YWCA	Young Women's Christian Association	

Contractions

auto	automobile	photo	photograph
bus	omnibus	piano	pianoforte
cello	violoncello	plane	aeroplane
exam	examination	pram	perambulator
gym	gymnasium	prom	promenade
mag	magazine	specs	spectacles
phone	telephone		

Exercises on Abbreviations

1. a) **What do the following abbreviations mean?**
        BSc, BBC, IDD, MP, PO, BC, MA, HRH, lbw, HMS
    b) **Often abbreviations are used in letter-writing. Give the meaning of the following:**
        a.m., inst., ult., Esq., Mr, p.m., St

2. **Give customary abbreviations for:**
    a) Monday, Tuesday, Wednesday, Friday, Saturday, January, February, August, September, October, November, December.
    b) Ounces, pounds (weight), hundredweights, pints, gallons, seconds, minutes, hours, inches, feet, yards, miles.
    c) Millimetres, centimetres, metres, kilometres, millilitres, centilitres, litres, milligrams, grammes, kilograms, millions.

3. **Write the following with all abbreviated terms in full:**
    a) Robt. Brown, Esq., 74 Abbey Rd, Glasgow, UK.
    b) Dr Thos. Smith, MP, a brother of the famous Harley St surgeon who recently toured the USA, was married on the 4th inst. in St Margaret's Chapel, Westminster.

4. **Write the following sentences, using the customary abbreviations:**
    a) William Miller of Her Majesty's Ship *Newcastle* was awarded the Victoria Cross for gallantry in action.
    b) Mister George Woods, a well-known local Justice of the Peace, was appointed managing director of Messieurs Cook and Company, Limited.

5. **Where contractions have been used in the following sentences, give the words in full:**
    a) We boarded a train as the bus was full.
    b) The specs were discovered in the pram.
    c) I saw his photo in a weekly mag.
    d) He phoned for news of the missing plane.
    e) The exam was held in the gym.

Antonyms

Words Opposite in Meaning

Give the words opposite in meaning to the following:

abroad	condemn	expand	here	motorist
absence	confined	failure	hero	mountain
accept	confirm	faint	heroic	moving
adult	contract	fair	hide	multiply
alive	correct	fair play	high	narrow
ancestor	coward	false	hollow	native
ancient	curse	familiar	home	near
answer	damp	famous	honest	never
arrive	dark	fancy	hot	new
asleep	day	far	humble	night
assemble	deep	fat	ignorant	noise
back	defeat	feeble	immense	none
backward	defend	fertile	inferior	north
bad	deny	few	innocent	nowhere
barren	depart	first	join	numerous
beautiful	depth	flow	junior	often
bent	die	foe	juvenile	old
better	difficult	foolish	land	opaque
big	dirty	foreign	last	open
bitter	disperse	found	late	out
black	divide	free	lean	past
bless	down	freedom	liberty	peace
bold	drunk	friend	light	pedestrian
bottom	dry	front	live	permanent
bow	dull	frown	long	plain
bright	dwarf	full	lost	pleasant
broad	early	future	loud	plural
buy	east	gaunt	love	polite
captive	easy	generous	low	poor
captivity	ebb	giant	mad	poverty
cheap	educated	go	maximum	powerful
chubby	empty	good	merry	praise
clean	enemy	guilty	minimum	present
clever	entrance	hard	minority	private
coarse	evening	hate	miser	prosperity
cold	ever	heavy	miserable	proud
come	everywhere	height	modern	purchase
conceal	exit	hell	morning	question ➤

50

quiet	shallow	spacious	tame	victory
rapid	short	spendthrift	temporary	wane
refuse	show	stale	there	war
retire	shut	stationary	these	wax
retreat	singular	steep	those	weak
reveal	slovenly	stern	timid	wealth
rich	slow	straight	tiny	west
right	small	strong	top	wet
rude	smart	stupid	transparent	white
sadness	smooth	success	truth	wild
safety	sober	summer	ugly	wise
seldom	soft	superior	unite	worse
selfish	solid	sweet	vacant	wrong
sell	sour	take	vague	young
senior	south	tall	valley	youth ❏

Give the words opposite in meaning to the following:

By adding a Prefix

advantage	direct	legible	order	safe
approve	essential	like	patient	sane
audible	fair	lock	perfect	screw
aware	famous	loyal	pleasure	selfish
behave	fire	modest	poisonous	sense
comfortable	happy	moral	polite	tidy
common	human	mortal	possible	transitive
connect	just	necessary	proper	trust
content	kind	noble	pure	twist
convenient	known	normal	regular	visible
correct	legal	obey	reverent	wise

By changing the Prefix

ascend, encourage, export, exterior, external, increase, inside.

By changing the Suffix

careful, cheerful, joyful, merciful, pitiful, useful.

The following may be said to be **Opposites**:

author	reader	judge	prisoner
detective	criminal	king	subject
doctor	patient	lawyer	client
driver	passenger	leader	follower
employer	employee	parent	child
gamekeeper	poacher	shopkeeper	customer
guardian	ward	speaker	listener
host	guest	teacher	pupil
hunter	quarry		

Exercises on Antonyms

1. Write words opposite in meaning to:

    success, visible, praise, transparent, fair play, arrive, nowhere, barren, ancient, wise.

2. Give the opposites (by prefix) of the following:

    audible, behave, known, legible, modest, noble, obedient, regular, sense, pleasant.

3. In the spaces provided write the opposites of each of the following:

    a) north   _South_
    b) entrance   _exit_
    c) rough   _smooth_
    d) pedestrian _motorist_
    e) guilty   _____

    f) possible   _impossible_
    g) often   _never_
    h) enemy   _friend_
    i) bitter   _sweet_
    j) senior   _junior_

4. Give the opposites of the adjectives in the following phrases:

    a) a bright boy
    b) a stormy day
    c) a wild boy

    d) a bright colour
    e) a stormy sea
    f) a wild horse

    g) a bright light
    h) a stormy meeting
    i) a wild flower

5. State the opposites of:

    a) an armed man
    b) I am sorry
    c) to keep step

    d) a false gift
    e) a heavy load
    f) to sing in tune

    g) a soft answer
    h) a mighty army
    i) she was dark

Exercises on Antonyms continued

6. In the spaces provided write the opposites of the words underlined:

Example: The ball was <u>solid</u> – hollow

a) It was a <u>beautiful</u> dress — *horrible*

b) Tuesday was a very <u>sunny</u> day — *rainy*

c) The <u>ascent</u> of the hill took two hours — *descent*

d) He has a <u>temporary</u> post — _____

e) She <u>purchased</u> the toy — *stole*

f) He is a <u>lazy</u> fellow — *smart*

g) There was an <u>abundance</u> of fruit — _____

h) He gave an <u>intelligent</u> answer — *stupid*

i) The sea was <u>rough</u> — *calm*

j) It was very <u>fertile</u> land — _____

7. Fill in the blanks in the following sentences with a word which is the opposite of the word underlined:

a) Read the <u>question</u> and then write your *answer*.

b) The polar bear which <u>escaped</u> from the zoo was soon *captured*

c) Last year the well was <u>empty</u> but this year it is *full*.

d) A <u>polite</u> boy is much thought of: there is nothing to be gained by being *rude*.

e) I suddenly <u>remembered</u> that I had *forgot* my spectacles.

8. Rewrite the following sentences, putting in words opposite in meaning to those underlined:

a) In the <u>morning</u> the sun <u>rises</u> in the <u>east</u>. *afternoon sets west*

b) The <u>hero</u> was <u>praised</u> for his <u>fair play</u>.

c) The <u>fancy</u> box was <u>big</u> and <u>heavy</u>.

d) <u>Profits</u> on <u>superior</u> articles made him <u>rich</u>.

e) The <u>mighty</u> army <u>advanced</u> after its <u>success</u>.

Synonyms

Words similar in meaning

abandon	leave	enormous	gigantic
abode	dwelling	extended	enlarged
abundant	plentiful	exterior	outside
accused	blamed	fall	drop
acute	sharp	famous	noted
adhere	stick	fatigue	weariness
affectionate	loving	feeble	weak
aid	help	gap	hole
ally	friend	glance	look
amazement	wonder	gravely	sternly
ancient	old	greeted	saluted
assemble	gather	grope	feel
astonish	surprise	gruff	harsh
asunder	apart	halt	stop
blank	empty	heroic	brave
bright	shining	hoax	trick
broad	wide	imitate	copy
caution	care	insolent	rude
circular	round	intention	purpose
coarse	rough	interior	inside
commence	begin	join	unite
comprehend	understand	lament	grieve
conceal	hide	lean	thin
constable	policeman	lofty	high
conversation	talk	loyal	true
courage	bravery	mad	insane
cunning	sly	malady	disease
curb	control	margin	edge
custom	habit	mariner	sailor
deceive	cheat	marsh	swamp
difficult	hard	maximum	most
disaster	calamity	meagre	scanty
dusk	twilight	minimum	least
elude	escape	moan	groan
emperor	king	modern	new
enemy	foe	moisture	dampness

mute	dumb	robust	strong
myth	fable	scene	sight
nimble	agile	shrine	tomb
noisy	rowdy	sleek	smooth
odour	smell	slender	slim
omen	sign	small	little
option	choice	squirming	wriggling
peculiar	strange	steed	horse
persuade	coax	stern	strict
plume	feather	stubborn	obstinate
powerful	strong	sturdy	strong
profit	gain	surrender	yield
prohibit	forbid	suspended	hung
prompt	quick	terror	fear
protect	guard	tested	tried
puny	weak	thrust	pushed
purchase	buy	tranquil	peaceful
quaint	odd	transparent	clear
quantity	amount	unite	join
queer	peculiar	vacant	empty
raiment	clothes	valour	bravery
ramble	roam	vanquish	defeat
rank	position	wealth	riches
rapid	quick	wicked	sinful
regret	sorrow	withdraw	retire
remedy	cure	wrath	anger
residence	dwelling	wretched	miserable
reveal	show	yearly	annually
roam	wander		

Exercises on Synonyms

1. Give words similar in meaning to the following:

comprehend, empty, sufficient, vicinity, attempted, enemies, risky, purchase,
perceive, modern.

(handwritten: understand, blank, ren, foes, buy)

Exercises on Synonyms continued

2. **In the spaces provided write words similar in meaning:**

a) bright   *shining*   f) peculiar   *strange*

b) convenient   g) lofty   *high*

c) disappear   h) unite   *join*

d) hoax   *trick*   i) margin   *edge*

e) valour   *bravery*   j) wrath   *anger*

3. **Place the words in their proper positions in the sentence:**

(handsome – pretty)   The *pretty* girl admired the *handsome* prince.

(proud – vain)   The *proud* king laughed at the *vain* little girl.

(fat – stout)   A *stout* woman should not eat *fat* meat.

(feeble – weak)   *Weak* tea will not refresh the *feeble* old lady.

(hot – sultry)   On a *hot* day don't drink *sultry* liquids.

(old – antique)   The *old* man was fond of *antique* furniture.

(loving – tender)   Her *loving* hands had prepared a *tender* chicken.

(sad – dull)   The day was *dull* and we felt quite *sad*.

4. **Give short sentences, one for each word, showing the correct use of the following:**

learn, teach; invent, discover; possible, probable; accept, except.

5. **Use similar words in place of the words underlined:**

a) The bucket <u>dropped</u> into the well. *fell*

b) "Don't <u>conceal</u> your real feelings." *hide*

c) I was <u>astonished</u> to find the house <u>vacant</u>. *surprised* *empty*

d) He <u>alters</u> his plans <u>annually</u>. *changes* *yearly*

Homonyms and Homophones

A **Homonym** is a word having the same sound, and perhaps the same spelling, as another, but with a different meaning. Where the spelling of the words is different the words may also be known as **Homophones** (sounding the same). The following homonyms are all of the homophone variety.

air	heir	flour	flower
aisle	isle, I'll	foul	fowl
allowed	aloud	gait	gate
ate	eight	gamble	gambol
bail	bale	gilt	guilt
ball	bawl	grate	great
bare	bear	groan	grown
beach	beech	hail	hale
bell	belle	hair	hare
blew	blue	hear	here
boar	bore	heard	herd
board	bored	higher	hire
bough	bow	him	hymn
boy	buoy	hoard	horde
buy	by, bye	hole	whole
ceiling	sealing	holy	wholly
cellar	seller	hour	our
cereal	serial	key	quay
cheap	cheep	knew	new
check	cheque	knight	night
coarse	course	knot	not
core	corps	knows	nose
council	counsel	leak	leek
crews	cruise	lightening	lightning
currant	current	loan	lone
dear	deer	loot	lute
die	dye	made	maid
draft	draught	mail	male
ewe	you, yew	main	mane
faint	feint	mare	mayor
fair	fare	meat	meet
feat	feet	medal	meddle
flew	flue		➤

missed	mist	scene	seen
muscle	mussel	scent	sent, cent
oar	ore	sea	see
pail	pale	seam	seem
pain	pane	sew	so, sow
pair	pare, pear	sight	site
pause	paws	soar	sore
peace	piece	sole	soul
peal	peel	son	sun
peer	pier	stair	stare
place	plaice	stake	steak
plain	plane	stationary	stationery
plum	plumb	steal	steel
pores	pours	stile	style
practice	practise	tail	tale
praise	prays, preys	tears	tiers
principal	principle	their	there
profit	prophet	threw	through
rains	reigns, reins	throne	thrown
raise	rays, raze	tide	tied
read	reed	time	thyme
real	reel	to	too, two
right, rite	wright, write	told	tolled
ring	wring	vain	vane, vein
road	rode, rowed	vale	veil
root	route	waist	waste
rose	rows	wait	weight
rye	wry	weak	week
sail	sale	wood	would ❏

Exercises   on Homonyms and Homophones

1. **Make short sentences, one for each word, showing the correct use of the following:**

   bear, bare, flower, flour, too, two, ate, eight, write, right.

Exercises on Homonyms and Homophones continued

2. **Cross out the wrong words:**

   She bought some (steak, ~~stake~~).
   The bicycle was for (~~sail~~, sale).
   We must (hire, ~~higher~~) a car.
   The (~~hole~~, whole) army marched into the town.
   The boy broke a (pane, ~~pain~~) of glass.
   We walked to the golf (~~coarse~~, course).
   (Their, ~~There~~) books are on the desks.
   The girl had to (wait, ~~weight~~) till four o'clock.
   The wounded soldier uttered a loud (~~grown~~, groan).
   The joiner (~~bored~~, board) a small (~~whole~~, hole) in the (wood, ~~would~~).

3. **Give sentences, one for each word, showing clearly the meaning of each of the following words:**

   pause, paws, steal, steel, heard, herd, reign, rain, their, there.

4. **Insert the words in their proper places:**

   (allowed – aloud)   It is not _allowed_ to speak _aloud_ in class.
   (maid – made)   The _Maid_ admitted that she had _made_ a mistake.
   (piece – peace)   He will give no _peace_ until he receives a _piece_ of cake.
   (scent – sent)   "Did you get the _scent_ I _sent_ you?"
   (stair– stare)   I saw him _stare_ at the man on the _stair_.
   (waist – waste)   "_Waste_ not, want not," said the woman with
                       the thin _waist_.

5. **Medal, horde, gambol, guilt, prophet, gamble, meddle, profit, gilt, hoard.**

   From the above list insert the correct words in the following sentences:

   A _____ of coins was found under the floor.
   The business man made a large _profit_ on the deal.
   He was told not to _meddle_ with the toys.
   I saw the lambs _____ in the field.
   His name was printed in large _____ letters.

Exercises on Homonyms and Homophones continued

6. The answers are words that are pronounced alike but differ in meaning, e.g.

	no	**nay**
	cry of a horse	**neigh**
a)	a female sheep	ewe
	an evergreen tree	yew
b)	sandy shore	beach
	kind of tree	beech
c)	guided	led
	a metal	lead
d)	opens lock	key
	harbour	quay
e)	flat land	plain
	joiner's tool	plane
f)	suffering	pain
	piece of glass	pane
g)	something round	ball
	shout loudly	bawl
h)	rough	coarse
	place for golf	course
i)	front of ship	bow
	branch of tree	bough
j)	gain	profit
	foretells future	prophet
k)	a flight of steps	stairs
	to look fixedly	stares
l)	sixty minutes	hour
	belonging to us	our
m)	quietness	peace
	a part of anything	piece
n)	a stupid person	fool
	no empty space	full
o)	in that place	there
	belonging to them	their

Verbs

Verbs are **doing** words we say, giving **doing** a very broad meaning. Words for **being done**, even **existing** (doing nothing) are verbs. Sometimes a verb consists of **one** word, sometimes of **two** or **more**, e.g.

a) Dogs *bark*.
b) Tom *laughed*.
c) *Is* Mary there?
d) *Go* away!
e) The day *will come*.
f) The jet *is landing*.

g) No words *were spoken*.
h) Guests *will be invited*.
i) The tiger *should have waited*.
j) My house *was being repaired*.
k) You *must have been joking*.

Note   One of the words in the verb is the **main** verb: the others are **auxiliaries** (helpers).

Underline the verbs in the following sentences:

1. Rain <u>fell</u> yesterday.
2. Day is <u>dawning</u>.
3. It <u>is</u> sunny today.
4. We have been <u>robbed</u>.
5. I do not <u>smoke</u>.
6. I could hardly <u>see</u>.

7. Uncle may be <u>coming</u> today.
8. We should have been <u>patient</u>.
9. You should not have been <u>told</u>.
10. They are not <u>looking</u> well.
11. The sheep were <u>worried</u> by dogs.
12. I was <u>worried</u> till you came.

Forms and Parts of Verbs Different forms have different uses, for e.g.

singular and plural subjects	A dog *barks*; dogs *bark*
different pronoun subjects	I *think*; he *thinks*
present, past, future tense (time)	I *walk*; I *walked*; I *shall walk*
continuous, completed action	We *are looking*; we *have looked*.

The **Infinitive** (e.g. *to bark*, *to look*) is the basic form from which most other parts of most verbs can be formed.

The **Present** and **Past Participles** are partly verb and partly adjective.

The **Present Participle** is formed by adding *-ing* to the infinitive and is used with parts of the verb *to be* to form continuous tenses, as in *We are looking* (look + *ing*).

The **Past Participle** is usually formed by adding *-ed* to the infinitive and is used with parts of the verb *to have* to form perfect (completed action) tenses, as in *We have looked* (look + *ed*). **Irregular** verbs form their past participle in other ways. Examples are listed below.

Some participles also serve purely as adjectives, e.g. A *dazzling* light; your story was *amusing*; my heart is *broken*; *cracked* cups.

Tenses   Except in the case of the verb *to be*, the **Present Tense** has the same form as the infinitive (unless the subject is *he*, *she*, *it* or a noun, when *-s* or *-es* is added). To form the **Future Tense** we place *shall* or *will* in front of the infinitive. To form the **Past Tense** of **regular** verbs we add *-ed* to the infinitive. So we have:

Infinitive	Present Tense	Future Tense	Past Tense
(to) look	(I, they) look	(I, we) shall look	(I, etc.) looked
	(he, it) looks	(you, etc.) will look	

Thus in **regular** verbs the same form serves both the **Past Tense**, (I) *looked*, and the **Past Participle** (I have) *looked*.

Many **irregular** verbs, however, form them differently. Here are a few of them:

Present Tense	Past Tense	Past Participle	Present Tense	Past Tense	Past Participle
am	was	been	choose	chose	chosen
arise	arose	arisen	come	came	come
drive	drove	driven	do	did	done
awake	awoke	awakened	drink	drank	drunk
bear	bore	borne	eat	ate	eaten
beat	beat	beaten	fall	fell	fallen
begin	began	begun	fly	flew	flown
ring	rang	rung	forget	forgot	forgotten
sing	sang	sung	freeze	froze	frozen
swim	swam	swum	give	gave	given
bite	bit	bitten	go	went	gone
hide	hid	hidden	lie	lay	lain
blow	blew	blown	ride	rode	ridden
grow	grew	grown	write	wrote	written
know	knew	known	run	ran	run
draw	drew	drawn	shake	shook	shaken
break	broke	broken	tear	tore	torn
speak	spoke	spoken			

Errors

One of the worst errors in speech (and writing) is the use of the Past Participle instead of the Past Tense (e.g. I *seen* you; they *done* that), and the Past Tense instead of the Past Participle (e.g. Have you *broke* it; they have *went*). To tune your ear to the correct usage give each of the above Past Tenses a subject (e.g. *Tom drove*) and say it aloud; then put a subject with *have*, *has* or *had* in front of the Past Participle (e.g. *I had* driven) and say it aloud.

Exercises on Verbs

1. Give the past tense of:

   arose   cut   kept   shook   bit
   arise, break, cut, fall, keep, say, shake, drink, bite, choose.
   broke   fell   said   drank   chose

2. Give the past participle of:

   bore   flown
   bear, drive, fly, give, hurt, ride, sell, speak, come, swim.
   driven   given   ridden   spoken   swum   *come*

3. Give the present tense of:

   eat   freeze   blow   awake   lose
   ate, beaten, froze, hidden, blew, spoken, awoke, sold, lost.
   beat   hide   speak   sell

4. a) Give the present participle of:

   throw, give, spring, fire, begin.

   b) Give the present infinitive of:

   burn, speak, stand, sweep, drive.

5. Give the past tense and past participle of:

   was done forgot   written sang   hid   gone began
   am, do, forget, grow, write, sing, tear, hide, go, begin.
   been did forgotten   wrote sung   hidden   went began

6. Complete the following table:

Present Tense	Past Tense	Past Participle
I rise	I rose	I have risen
I forget	I forgot	I have forgotten
I cut	I cut	I have cut
I sing	I sang	I have sung
I blow	I blew	I have blown

7. Fill in each space correctly with one of these words:

   rise, rose, raise, risen, raised.
   a) He _raised_ his hand to greet his friend.
   b) Yesterday the boy _rose_ at five o'clock.
   c) I saw him _rise_ from his seat.
   d) She tried to _raise_ the lid.
   e) The sun had _risen_ in the sky.

8. Use the correct part of the verbs in the blank spaces:

   (go)   She had _gone_ for a walk.
   (see)   He _saw_ his uncle yesterday.
   (fall)   The old man _fell_ asleep in his chair.
   (awake) He was _awakened_ by the noise.
   (dream) The boy was _dreaming_ about pirates.

In each of the sentences below there are groups of two words within brackets. One of the two words is correct, the other wrong. Underline the correct word.

1. We (drank, drunk) our tea before we (sung, sang) the carol.

2. After he had (ran, run) about 5 kilometres, he (sank, sunk) to the ground.

3. Some cloth is (wove, woven) from wool which has (grown, grew) on sheep.

4. He had (gave, given) me the parcel before he was (took, taken) a prisoner.

5. The timid creature was (drove, driven) into a narrow valley where it was (slew, slain) by the cruel tiger.

6. The vessel (sank, sunk) before they had (swam, swum) a great distance.

7. The tree had (fell, fallen) across the road and many of its branches were (broke, broken).

8. By the time the sun had (rose, risen) the aeroplane had (flown, flew) across the sea.

9. No sooner had he (spoke, spoken) than a deer (sprang, sprung) into our path.

10. He (began, begun) to look for the toy which he had (gave, given) to his brother.

11. The man had (threw, thrown) away the purse which was (stole, stolen) from the lady.

12. The jacket had been well (wore, worn) and the cloth had (shrank, shrunk).

13. After we had (ate, eaten) our supper we went to the pond which was (froze, frozen) over.

14. The picture was (drawn, drew) by a famous and wealthy artist who had (rose, risen) from poverty.

15. They had just (went, gone) when we were (saw, seen) by our friends.

16. A nest had (fell, fallen) to the ground, where it had been (blew, blown) by the wind.

17. The bell (rang, rung) just after I had (wrote, written) the letter.

Adjectives

An **Adjective** is a word which qualifies or adds to the meaning of a noun. (An old form for **Adjective** was **Ad-noun**.)

Adjectives may be divided into three main classes.

1. Descriptive Adjectives

Good, bad, hard, soft, old, young, pale, red.
Example: The **old** man caught a **bad** cold.

2. Adjective of Quantity

a) **Definite** (including numerals)

One, seven, twenty, second, fifth, both, double.
Example: **Both** players scored **three** goals in the **second** game.

b) **Indefinite**

All, any, few, many, much, several, some.
Example: We met **several** boys who had caught **some** fish.

3. Adjectives of Distinction

a) **Demonstrative**

This, that, these, those, yon, yonder.
Example: **This** stone was found on **yonder** hill.

b) **Interrogative**

Which, what, whose.
Example: **Which** book do you want?

c) **Distributive**

Each, every, either, neither.
Example: He could go home by **either** route.

Exercises on Adjectives

Underline the **Adjectives** in the following sentences:

1. The tall gentleman wore a blue overcoat.

2. Little Jim was a delicate boy with pale cheeks.

3. The weather was wet and foggy.

4. The ugly old witch spoke in a hoarse cracked voice.

5. The lost ball was found near the wooden gate.

Comparison of Adjectives

Adjectives can have three *degrees*: **Positive**, **Comparative**, **Superlative**.

The **Positive** is simply descriptive, describing a noun or pronoun, e.g. a *short* holiday; *beautiful* hats; *clever* pupils; this is *broken*.

The **Comparative** is used in comparing some creature, thing or group with **one** other (creature, thing or group). e.g. the *taller* of the two; *taller* than the rest; mice are *smaller* than rats. If the positive is a short word the comparative is usually formed by adding *-er* to the positive, e.g. fast-er; great-er.

The **Superlative** is used in comparing some creature, thing or group with **more than one** other, e.g. the *tallest* of the three; the *wisest* of men. It is usually formed by adding *-est* to the positive, if a short word. When one thing or creature is compared with more than one other **treated as a group**, the comparative is used, e.g. Tom is *taller* than *the rest of the class*.

Adjectives of three syllables or more and most adjectives of two syllables form their comparative by placing *more* in front of the positive, and the superlative by placing *most* in front.

Some adjectives have quite different words for the comparative and superlative.

Positive	Comparative	Superlative	Positive	Comparative	Superlative
a) Small word in positive					
big	bigger	biggest	late	later	latest
fast	faster	fastest	long	longer	longest
happy	happier	happiest	small	smaller	smallest
great	greater	greatest	tall	taller	tallest
clever	cleverer	cleverest	narrow	narrower	narrowest
b) Different word for comparative and superlative					
bad	worse	worst	little	less	least
far	farther	farthest	many	more	most
good	better	best	much	more	most

Positive	Comparative	Superlative
c) Longer word in positive		
beautiful	more beautiful	most beautiful
careful	more careful	most careful
comfortable	more comfortable	most comfortable
ignorant	more ignorant	most ignorant

Exercises on Comparison of Adjectives

1. Give the comparatives and superlatives of:

   many, hot, bad, famous, little.

2. Write the comparatives of:

   fast, good, gracious, tall, beautiful.

3. Write the superlatives of:

   thin, much, comfortable, handsome.

4. Complete the following table:

Positive	Comparative	Superlative
long	longer	longest
far	farther	farthest
good	better	best
generous	more generous	most generous
late	later	latest
cautious	more cautious	most cautious

5. State whether the following words are positive, comparative or superlative:

   nearest, better, far, more certain, surest, larger, most wonderful, bad, shorter, biggest.

6. Correct the following sentences:
   a) James was the biggest of the twins.
   b) A more kinder lady you could not meet.
   c) The best team won the football match.
   d) Fred was the most fast of all the runners.
   e) Who is the tallest, Jack or Betty?
   f) He proved to be the ignorantest person.
   g) Of the two, I like George best.
   h) A badder boy I have never known.
   i) The sailor lifted the thinnest end of the rope.
   j) The patient made the wonderfulest recovery.

Adverbs

An **Adverb** is a word which modifies or adds to the meaning of a verb, an adjective, or another adverb.

Adverbs may be divided, according to their use, into the following classes:

a) **Time** – before, now, since, then, already, soon, seldom.
   Example: We have met **before**.

b) **Place** – here, there, everywhere, nowhere.
   Example: They came **here** yesterday.

c) **Manner** – badly, easily, slowly, well.
   Example: The tall boy won **easily**.

d) **Degree** – almost, much, only, quite, very, rather.
   Example: The old lady walked **very** slowly.

e) **Number** – once, twice.
   Example: They ran **twice** round the park.

f) **Questioning** – where, when, how.
   Example: **When** did you see him?

g) **Affirmation** and **Negation** – yes, certainly, no, not.
   Example: She can **certainly** swim.
                   I have **not** read the book.

(Many adverbs are often used as connecting words and therefore become conjunctions. You will read about them on page 85.)

The majority of Adverbs are formed from corresponding Adjectives by adding "-ly", e.g. quickly, bravely, seriously, happily, clearly, slowly, quietly, angrily, fatally, suitably.

Exercises | on Adverbs

Underline the **Adverbs** in the following sentences:

1. Dinner will soon be ready.
2. There lay the object of our search.
3. The man walked slowly across the field.
4. The apples were quite good.
5. I once saw an eagle kill a rabbit.
6. Where did you find that knife?
7. He can certainly boast about his adventures.
8. The story ended happily.

Comparison of Adverbs

Adverbs are compared in the same way as **Adjectives**. As most adverbs are two-syllable words or longer they generally form the Comparative and Superlative by adding **more** and **most** to the Positive.

	Positive	Comparative	Superlative
Regular (i)			
	early	earlier	earliest
	fast	faster	fastest
	long	longer	longest
	soon	sooner	soonest
Regular (ii)			
	bitterly	more bitterly	most bitterly
	bravely	more bravely	most bravely
	briefly	more briefly	most briefly
	carefully	more carefully	most carefully
	clearly	more clearly	most clearly
	cruelly	more cruelly	most cruelly
	easily	more easily	most easily
	freely	more freely	most freely
	greedily	more greedily	most greedily
	happily	more happily	most happily
	loudly	more loudly	most loudly
	quickly	more quickly	most quickly
	slowly	more slowly	most slowly
	willingly	more willingly	most willingly
Irregular			
	badly	worse	worst
	far	farther	farthest
	forth	further	furthest
	ill	worse	worst
	late	later	last
	much	more	most
	well	better	best

Some Common Verbs with Suitable Adverbs

Verbs	Adverbs
acted	quickly, suddenly, warily
answered	correctly, immediately, angrily
ate	greedily, hungrily, quickly, slowly
bled	freely, profusely, slightly
bowed	humbly, respectfully, stiffly
caressed	fondly, gently, lovingly
charged	bravely, desperately, furiously
chuckled	artfully, gleefully, happily
crept	quietly, silently, softly, stealthily
decided	carefully, eventually, immediately
explained	briefly, clearly, concisely
fell	heavily, quickly, suddenly
flogged	brutally, cruelly, unmercifully
fought	bravely, furiously, gamely
frowned	angrily, sulkily
injured	accidentally, fatally, seriously, slightly
left	hurriedly, quietly, suddenly
listened	anxiously, attentively, carefully
lost	badly, heavily, sportingly
mumbled	angrily, inaudibly, indistinctly
pondered	deeply, seriously, thoughtfully
pulled	hastily, strongly, vigorously
ran	hurriedly, quickly, rapidly, slowly
remembered	clearly, distinctly, faintly, slightly
sang	loudly, softly, sweetly, tunefully
shone	brightly, brilliantly, clearly, dimly
shouted	frantically, joyfully, jubilantly, loudly, suddenly
slept	fitfully, lightly, soundly
smiled	broadly, happily, ruefully
sneered	insolently, impudently, tauntingly
spent	foolishly, freely, recklessly, sparingly
spoke	clearly, distinctly, earnestly, loudly, plainly, slowly
sprang	hurriedly, lightly, quickly, suddenly
staggered	awkwardly, drunkenly, weakly
strove	bravely, desperately, manfully
stuttered	excitedly, haltingly, painfully
trembled	fearfully, frightfully, visibly
waited	patiently, anxiously

Verbs	Adverbs
walked	clumsily, haltingly, quickly, slowly, smartly
wept	bitterly, distractedly, sadly, touchingly
whispered	audibly, quietly, softly
yielded	stubbornly, weakly, willingly

Exercises   on Adverbs

1. In the spaces provided place the following adverbs:

heavily, furiously, silently, soundly, immediately, sparingly, broadly, patiently.

He charged	_furiously_	He decided	_immediately_
He slept	_soundly_	He crept	_silently_
He spent	_sparingly_	He fell	_heavily_
He smiled	_broadly_	He waited	_patiently_

2. Add any suitable adverb to the following sentences:

The girl sings	_loudly_	The clerk wrote	_neatly_
The lion roars	_boldly_	The river flows	_quickly_
The artist paints	_carefully_	The stars shine	_beautifully_
The child sleeps	_silently_	The horse gallops	_gracefully_
The cat walks	_slowly_	The man frowns	_sadly_

3. Give the comparatives and superlatives of:

soon, briefly, well, early, clearly.

4. Write the comparatives of:

long, badly, carefully, late, freely.

5. State the superlatives of:

fast, quickly, sick, easily, forth.

6. Complete the following table:

Positive	Comparative	Superlative
long	_longer_	_longest_
happily	_happier_	_happiest_
late	_latest_	_latest_
willingly	_more willingly_	_most willingly_
ill	_worse_	_worst_

Word Building

Form Nouns from:

able	civilise	famous	magic	sad
absent	clean	favourite	manly	satisfy
abundant	collect	feed	marry	scene
accurate	commence	fierce	merry	school
acquaint	compare	fly	mission	scientific
act	conclude	fragrant	mock	secure
admire	confident	free	moral	see
adopt	confuse	friend	mountain	select
advertise	content	grand	move	serene
allow	create	great	music	serve
amuse	credit	grow	occupy	shade
angry	cruel	happy	oppose	sick
anxious	curious	hate	persuade	simple
appear	dark	hero	please	speak
applaud	deceive	high	proclaim	steal
apply	decent	holy	profess	stream
approve	decide	imagine	prosper	strike
arrive	deep	imitate	proud	strong
ascend	defend	inform	prove	succeed
assist	depart	injure	provide	superior
attend	describe	interfere	punctual	tell
attract	destroy	introduce	punish	think
bag	develop	invent	pursue	thrive
beautiful	discover	invite	ready	typical
beg	divide	judge	real	vain
begin	do	just	rebel	various
behave	encourage	know	receive	visit
believe	enjoy	laugh	recognise	war
bitter	enter	lazy	relieve	warm
boy	equal	learn	remember	weak
brave	exceed	like	renew	weary
breathe	exhaust	listen	repeat	weigh
bright	expect	live	repent	wide
cash	explain	long	resent	wise
child	faithful	lose	reveal	worthy
choose	false	loyal	revive	young

Form Adjectives from:

ability	critic	heat	notice	strength
accident	cruelty	height	oak	study
admire	custom	hero	obey	success
adventure	danger	hope	occasion	sun
affection	deceive	imagine	oppose	sympathy
angel	decide	industry	ornament	talk
anger	describe	inform	parent	terror
anxiety	destroy	introduce	patience	thirst
athlete	disaster	iron	peace	thought
attract	distance	Italy	peril	tide
autumn	duty	joy	person	tire
beauty	energy	law	picture	trouble
bible	enjoy	learn	pity	truth
boy	exceed	length	please	type
brass	expression	life	poet	union
breath	faith	love	poison	value
Britain	fame	luxury	pride	vanity
care	fashion	man	prosper	variety
caution	father	marvel	quarrel	victory
centre	fault	meddle	rag	voice
change	favour	melody	reason	volcano
charity	fire	mercy	science	Wales
child	five	metal	sense	war
choir	fool	mine	shadow	water
choose	force	mischief	shower	wave
circle	forget	mock	silk	weary
collect	fortune	mountain	silver	west
colony	France	mourn	sister	winter
comfort	friend	move	skill	wisdom
conclude	giant	music	sorrow	wit
continent	girl	mystery	south	wood
courage	gold	nation	spire	wool
coward	grace	nature	spirit	worth
craft	grief	neglect	star	wretch
credit	harm	noise	stop	year
crime	hate	north	storm	youth

Form Verbs from:

able	courage	frost	long	shelf
actor	creator	full	magnet	short
banishment	critic	glass	moisture	simple
bath	custom	glory	nation	soft
beauty	dark	gold	obedience	solution
blood	deed	grass	peril	song
bright	description	grief	pleasure	spark
broad	dictation	growth	proof	speech
camp	education	horror	provision	strong
circle	false	imitation	pure	success
circulation	fat	joy	relief	terror
civil	fertile	just	resident	thought
clean	fine	knee	resolution	tight
cloth	food	knowledge	rich	tomb
colony	force	large	roll	trial
composition	friend	life	sharp	wide

Form Adverbs from:

ability	happy	joy	sweet	true
critic	heavy	pure	terror	weary
faith	horror	simple	thought	wide

Compound Words

A word in its simplest form is called a **Primary Word**, e.g. table, board, egg. If we combine two Primary Words to form one word we get a **Compound Word**, e.g. tablecloth, blackboard, eggcup.

Form Compound Words from the following:

ache	cup	guard	maid	pot	strong
ball	day	gun	man	room	table
black	door	hat	master	safe	tea
board	dust	heart	mat	school	time
boot	egg	house	milk	servant	tomb
cart	fall	jam	mill	shed	tooth
church	fire	lace	out	shop	thrift
cloth	fly	lamp	pick	son	water
coal	foot	life	piece	spend	wife
craft	gentle	light	pond	stand	witch
cry	grand	load	post	stone	yard

Exercises on Word Building

1. Make a noun corresponding to each of the following words:

   a) please   *[pleasant pleasure]*   f) encourage   *[encouragement]*
   b) prove   *[proven proof]*   g) strong   *[strength]*
   c) know   *[known knowledge]*   h) real   *[reality]*
   d) proud   *[pride]*   i) just   *[justice]*
   e) choose   *[chosen choice]*   j) give   *[gave gift]*

2. Give nouns formed from:

   [selection, baggage reader, successful dividend]
   select, grow, bag, act, receive, invite, succeed, repent, divide.

3. By adding a suffix, form a noun from each of the following:

   [growth, actor, imitation, repentance]
   [ment, ice, ism, ery, ance, dom, ant, ty, ion, ness]
   astonish, coward, critic, trick, assist, free, inform, loyal, invent, sick.

4. Make an adjective corresponding to each of the following words:

   [heated, angry, high, boyish, senseless]
   Britain, heat, expense, anger, faith, height, fashion, boy, vanity, sense.
   [British, expensive, faithful, fashionable, vain, endless]

5. Give adjectives from:

   a) decide   *[decided]*   f) mystery   *[mysterious]*
   b) bible   *[biblical]*   g) voice   *[voiceless]*
   c) talk   *[talkative]*   h) nation   *[national]*
   d) circle   *[circular]*   i) winter   *[wintry]*
   e) attract   *[attractive]*   j) peril   *[perilous]*

6. Give a verb corresponding to each of the following words:

   Example: Solution – **solve**.

   a) knee   *[greening]*   f) tight   *[tighten]*
   b) strong   *[strengthen]*   g) grief   *[grieve]*
   c) description   *[describe]*   h) large   *[enlarge]*
   d) gold   *[gild]*   i) glory   *[glorify]*
   e) custom   *[accustom]*   j) food   *[feed]*

7. Give verbs from:

   obedient, sweet, education, fat, life, composition, civil, tomb, bath, pure.

Exercises on Word Building continued

8. Form adverbs from:

anger, tune, excitement, freedom, anxiety, frantic, worry, serious, fool, silence.

9. Complete the following compound words:

black board   milk *bottle*   grand *father*
hat ~~stand~~ *land*   *butter* cup   *lamp* post
lamp *shade*   *dish* cloth   *foot* ball
tooth *fairy*   book *shop*   *foot* stool

10. Complete the following table:

Adjective	Noun	Verb
long	length	lengthen
strong	*strength*	*strengthen*
broad	*breadth*	*broaden*
glad	*gladness*	*gladen*
able	*ability*	*enable*
wide	*width*	*widen*

11. Make sentences, two for each word, using the following words
    a)   as nouns;
    b)   as adjectives:

brick, chief, diamond, garden, iron, light, music, sole, square, summer, young.

12. Write sentences, two for each word, using each of the following words first as a noun and then as a verb:

brush, cycle, fire, heat, hope, notice, sail, saw, spring, step, turn, wave.

13. What part of speech is the word **round** in each of the following sentences?
    a)   It was a large **round** table.   *adjective*
    b)   The tourist played a **round** of golf.   *noun*
    c)   The speaker turned **round**.   *adverb*
    d)   The boy ran quickly **round** the field.   *noun*
    e)   The horses must **round** this corner.   *preposition*

Concord

Concord means agreement or harmony. In grammar we apply this word as meaning perfect agreement between subject and verb. This is shown by the subject and verb having the same person and number.

1. When the **subject** is **singular**, the **verb** is **singular**, e.g.
   a) He writes.
   b) She swims.
   c) The baby cries.

2. When the **subject** is **plural**, the **verb** is **plural**, e.g.
   a) We write.
   b) They swim.
   c) The babies cry.

3. Expressions such as **each of**, **one of**, **neither of**, **every one of**, **not one of** and words such as **each**, **every**, **none**, **anybody**, **everybody** and **nobody** must be followed by **verbs** in the **singular**, e.g.
   a) **Each of** the boys **has** a toy.
   b) **One of** the ladies **is** married.
   c) **Neither of** the brothers **was** present.
   d) **Is either of** the sisters coming?
   e) **Every one of** us **knows** that it is wrong.
   f) **Not one of** the girls **has** a skipping rope.
   g) **Each** man **was** searched.
   h) **Every** child **has** a secret ambition.
   i) **Anybody is** admitted to the caves.
   j) **Everybody was** delighted at the close.
   k) **Nobody is** displeased with the result.
   l) **None** of the ships **was** lost.

4. A **singular subject** with attached phrases introduced by **with** or **like** or **as well as** is followed by a **singular verb**, e.g.
   a) The boy, **with** several others, **was** late for school.
   b) Alice, **like** Rose, **is** tall for her age.
   c) Tom, **as well as** Fred, **rises** early in the morning.

5. When a **verb** has **two singular subjects** connected by **and** the verb is **plural**, e.g.
   a) The cat **and** the dog **were** great friends.
   b) The farmer **and** his wife **are** jolly people.

6. When a **verb** has **one or more plural subjects** connected by **and**, the **verb** is **plural**, e.g.
   a) The officer **and** his men **were** crossing the field.
   b) The boys **and** the girls **are** sure of their work.

7. **Two singular subjects** separated by "either _____ or", "neither _____ nor" take a **singular verb**, e.g.
   a) **Either** one **or** the other **has** blundered.
   b) **Either** he **or** she **is** right.
   c) **Neither** Grace **nor** Helen **knows** anything about it.
   d) **Neither** he **nor** she **writes** well.

8. Subjects separated by "either (*plural*) or", "neither (*plural*) nor", "both _____ and", also "all _____ but", take a plural verb, e.g.
   a) **Either** the boys or the girls **are** to blame.
   b) **Neither** the pirates **nor** the sailors **were** afraid of battle.
   c) **Both** Hugh **and** Sam **were** standing.
   d) **All but** James **are** going to the picnic.
   e) **All of** them **but** Grace **are** correct.

Exercises   on Concord

In each of the sentences below there are groups of two words within brackets. One of the two words is correct, the other wrong. Underline the correct word:

1. Each of the boys (is, are) going on holiday so each of them (has, have) gone to bed early.
2. Everybody (was, were) pleased as each of them (was, were) treated alike.
3. Neither he nor she (want, wants) to go.
4. (Wasn't, Weren't) we sorry when we heard you (was, were) going?
5. One of the men (is, are) married and so he (get, gets) preference.
6. All but William (has, have) behaved well so all but William (get, gets) away early.
7. James, as well as John, (rise, rises) at eight, so James, like John, (is, are) early for work.
8. Neither of the singers (was, were) present.
9. Every little girl (desire, desires) a nice doll.
10. The miller and his wife (is, are) a happy couple.
11. Why (does, do) every one of us (do, does) stupid things at times?

Exercises   on Concord continued

12. Neither of them (has, <u>have</u>) failed as both of them (is, <u>are</u>) right in five sums.
13. The girl, with several others, (was, <s>were</s>) going to school.
14. Both Agnes and Albert (is, <u>are</u>) here tonight.
15. Either Fred or Jean (<u>has</u>, have) made a mistake, so either he or she (<u>is</u>, are) wrong.
16. Not one of the boys (<u>has</u>, have) a knife although not one of the boys (<u>is</u>, are) young.
17. John, like James, (<u>is</u>, are) smaller than Peter.
18. (Is, <u>Are</u>) Frank and Margaret happy, as both he and she (was, <u>were</u>) complaining?
19. All of you but Andrew (is, <u>are</u>) good, so all of you but Andrew (get, <u>gets</u>) a reward.
20. Each of the ladies (is, <u>are</u>) delighted as each of the ladies (receive, <u>receives</u>) a prize.
21. Anybody (<u>is</u>, are) allowed to enter.
22. Every one of us (know, <u>knows</u>) the answers because every one of us (was, <u>were</u>) copying.
23. Nobody (<u>is</u>, are) grumpy at the camp because nobody (<u>is</u>, are) allowed to feel lonely.
24. Arthur, as well as Donald, (<u>is</u>, are) clever, so Arthur, as well as Donald, (<u>has</u>, have) succeeded.
25. The gentlemen and the ladies (was, <u>were</u>) wearing evening dress.
26. Either one or the other (<u>is</u>, are) wealthy as either one or the other (<u>has</u>, have) plenty of money.
27. All of us but David (was, <u>were</u>) on holiday so all of us but David (is, <u>are</u>) feeling relaxed.
28. (Wasn't, <u>Weren't</u>) they pleased when they heard we (was, <u>were</u>) coming?
29. Cecil, as well as Annie, (like, <u>likes</u>) spelling and Cecil, as well as Annie, (hate, <u>hates</u>) arithmetic.
30. Either Flora or Richard (<u>has</u>, have) measles, so either she or he (<u>is</u>, are) in bed.
31. Why (do, <u>does</u>) every one of them do that, when every one of them (know, <u>knows</u>) the arrangements?

Pronouns

There are **Personal**, **Relative**, **Interrogative**, **Demonstrative** and **Indefinite** Pronouns. Pronouns stand **for** (pro-) nouns.

Personal Pronouns and some Relative and Interrogative Pronouns have a **Nominative** form when they are the subject of a verb, an **Objective** form when they are the object of a verb (or preposition) and a **Possessive** form. Personal pronouns also distinguish the **First Person** (the person(s) speaking, i.e. I or we), the **Second Person** (the person(s) spoken to, i.e. you) and the **Third Person** (the person(s) spoken about). So we have:

Personal Pronouns

Person	Nominative	Objective	Possessive	Reflexive	(Possessive Adjective)
First (Sing.)	I	me	mine	myself	(my)
Second (Sing.)	you	you	yours	yourself	(your)
Third (Sing.)	he	him	his	himself	(his)
	she	her	hers	herself	(her)
	it	it	its	itself	(its)
First (Plur.)	we	us	ours	ourselves	(our)
Second (Plur.)	you	you	yours	yourselves	(your)
Third (Plur.)	they	them	theirs	themselves	(their)

Note 1   The reflexive form is used in two ways, a) reflexive, b) intensive, e.g.
   I have cut myself. He blames himself. (Reflexive.)
   I myself was unaware of that. (Intensive, emphatic.)

Note 2   The reflexives do not have different forms for nominative, objective or possessive. It is wrong to say *hisself* or *theirselves*.

Note 3   A *possessive adjective* simply describes a noun, e.g. *your* pencil.
   The *possessive of a pronoun* stands for a noun, e.g.
   This pencil is *yours* (i.e. *your pencil*).
   He's a friend of *ours* (i.e. from among *our friends*).

Nominative and **Objective** forms – correct use.

The **nominative** forms of pronouns must be used for subjects of verbs.

I bought some apples.	*We* saw a large cave.
You will catch a cold.	*They* shouted with joy.
He caught a fish.	*She* sang a song.

The objective forms must be used for objects of verbs or prepositions.

The play bored *me*.   The children left *us*.

The animal stared *at me*.   Go and run *after them*.

Special case – Complement of the verb *to be*.

The verb *to be* does not take an object. When we say "That is nonsense", the word *nonsense* is called the complement (or 'completion') of the verb *is*.

It *is I* who am the master of my fate   (*I* is the complement of *is*).

It *was they*, not *we*, who ran away   (*they*, *we* complements of *was*).

Mistakes are common when *that* is used for *who*, e.g.

It was *them*, not *us*, *that* ran away (wrong).

In the first sentence we could even have two mistakes:

It is *me* that *is* the master of my fate (*me*, *is*, both wrong).

Exception: If someone asks "Who is there?" the answer "It is *me*" is now accepted in practice, though "It is I" is the grammatically correct form.

Note It is not only the simple parts of the verb *to be* which have a complement, e.g.

It *appears to be they* who are refusing.

Double Nominatives and Objectives

The above rules – **nominative for the subject** (and for the complement of the verb *to be*), **objective for the object** (of a verb or preposition) – apply also where there is more than one subject or object, e.g. two pronouns, or a noun and a pronoun.

Examples:

She and *I* can't agree.   It suits both *them* and *us*.

It's *you* and *I* who lose.   Between *you* and *me*, he's mad.

Errors:

It's *you* and *me* who lose.   Between *you* and *I*, he's mad.

Other Errors to Avoid

a) After *as* and *than*.

(Wrong.) He is as tall as me.   (Correct.) He is as tall as *I* (am).

(Wrong.) He is taller than me.   (Correct.) He is taller than *I* (am).

Note these sentences, however:

She likes you as much as *me*. ⎤   Both correct. Means "as much as
She likes you more than *me*. ⎦   (more than) she likes *me*".

She likes you as much as *I*. ⎤   Both correct. Means "as much as
She likes you more than *I*. ⎦   (more than) I like you".

b) *Spelling* of *its* (pronoun) and *it's*.

Its is the possessive of *it* (with no apostrophe), e.g. This class has forgotten *its* manners.

It's stands for *it is* (or *it has*). The apostrophe denotes omissions, e.g. *It's* dry today, but *it's* been wet recently.

Relative Pronouns

A relative pronoun (*who, whom, whose, which, what, that*) joins two parts of a sentence, standing in one part for a noun or pronoun mentioned in the other part, and referring to that noun or pronoun, which is called its **antecedent**, e.g.

Tom is a boy *who* learns fast.   That's a job *of which* I'm proud.
She is a pupil *whom* I taught.   This is the house *that* Jack built.
Was it he *whose* boat sank?   *What* is to be, will be.

Sometimes a relative pronoun is omitted and has to be 'understood', e.g.

That's a girl ≠ I taught last year.   The shop ≠ I went to was shut.

Sometimes the pronoun includes its own antecedent, e.g.

Who steals my purse steals trash.   (*who = he, who* …)
What will be, will be.   (*what = that, which* …)

Who, whom refer only to persons (singular or plural):

who, the nominative, must be used only for the subject of a verb,

whom, the objective, must always be used for the object of a verb or preposition, e.g. Is there anyone *whom* we can trust? It is wrong to say: Is there anyone *who* we can trust?

Whose, that can refer to persons, animals or things, singular or plural.

Which is used to refer to animals and things (singular or plural) but not to persons. Its possessive form is either *whose* or *of which*.

What is seldom used as a relative pronoun, though it is common as an interrogative. It is sometimes wrongly used instead of *that*, e.g.

This is the book *what* I lost (wrong).
This is the book *that* I lost (correct).

Interrogative Pronouns

Interrogative Pronouns (*who? whom? whose? which? what?*) ask a question.
They refer to persons, animals and things just as when used as relative pronouns.

It is a common mistake to use *who?* (the nominative form) in sentences where *whom?* (the objective) is required, e.g.

Who do you think I met? (wrong)

Whom do you think I met? (*Whom* is the object of *met*) (correct)

Note *Who* do you think you are? is correct. (*Are* is part of the verb *to be*, which does not take an object.)

Demonstrative Pronouns

A Demonstrative Pronoun (*this, that, these, those*) 'points out' what it stands for, e.g.

This is intolerable.	I like *that*.	He is like *that* sometimes.
I prefer *these* to *those*.	*That's* better.	Is it as serious as *that*?

Note 1 *This* and *these*, when opposed to *that* and *those* in a sentence, usually distinguish what is nearer, more recent, or more recently mentioned, from what is more distant in place or time, e.g.

That was nonsense: the truth is *this* . . .

Note 2 The words *this, that, these, those* are, of course, also used as (demonstrative) adjectives, when they point out *and* describe a noun in a sentence, or one that is understood, e.g.

This house is bigger than *that* (house).

That is the wrong door. (*door* is understood after *that*.)

Indefinite Pronouns

An Indefinite Pronoun stands for some person(s) or thing(s) unspecified, e.g.

Tell me *more*.	You don't know *much*.	*Both* owned up.
Either will do.	*One* must remember.	*None* returned.
Take *any* of them.	Give me a black *one*; I dislike white *ones*.	

Note 1 A singular indefinite pronoun should not be referred to as if it were a plural. This is a very common error, e.g.

Everyone must pay *their* fair share (wrong).

Everyone must pay *his* fair share (correct).

Everyone must pay *his* or *her* fair share (correct).

Note 2 Another common error is to switch from the indefinite *one* to another pronoun, e.g.

One must not miss *his* chance (wrong).

One must not miss *one's* chance (correct).

Exercises   on Pronouns

Complete these sentences using the correct word from each pair in brackets:

1. (He, Him) and (I, me) went for a walk.
2. It was (he, him) (who, whom) we saw in the shop.
3. No one believes it was (she, her); everyone thinks it was (I, me).
4. Between (he, him) and (I, me) we ate the whole cake.
5. (She, Her) and (I, me) can go, but you and (he, him) cannot.
6. Jack is not as clever as (he, him) or (I, me).
7. It seems to be (they, them) (who, whom) the police suspect.
8. (Her, She) and you sang very well together.
9. John is much brighter than (he, him) or (I, me).
10. This discovery must remain a secret between you and (I, me).
11. It's not for (we, us) to run after (they, them).
12. It was (he, him) who knew the right answer.
13. (Who, Whom) are (they, them)?
14. (We, Us) lads were at the cinema at the same time as (they, them).
15. Between you and (I, me), I know all about Sue and (she, her).
16. He is almost as big as (I, me) but smaller than (she, her).
17. Her sisters are smaller than (we, us) but she is taller than (I, me).
18. You must choose between (they, them) and (we, us).
19. You and (I, we) could do it, but not you and (he, him).
20. It appears to be (she, her) about (who, whom) you should worry.
21. (She, Her) and (I, me) are twelve years of age.
22. Her cousin is younger than (she, her) or (I, me).
23. Was it (I, me) (who, whom) you saw there?
24. I spoke to (he, him) and (she, her) about (who, whom) to tell.
25. We are certain it was not (he, him) (who, whom) was to blame.
26. It is not (she, her) that I am angry with, but (he, him).
27. (He, Him) I can excuse, but not (they, them).
28. Was it (he, him) or (she, her) who found the purse?
29. (Who, Whom) do you think we met?
30. Anyone (who's, whose) poor shouldn't buy one of (them, these).
31. That's not your pencil. (Its, It's) (mine, mine's).
32. Everyone (what, that) wants a ticket, must bring (their, his) money.
33. Neither he nor she (know, knows) what (they, he or she) (is, are) doing.
34. Let's go, you and (I, me), and see (who's, whose) (there, their).
35. (Who, Whom) were you speaking to?

Conjunctions

A Conjunction joins words, phrases or sentences together.

There are two main kinds of conjunction:

1. Conjunctions which join similar parts of speech and clauses of equal value, e.g.

and, both … and, but, for, whereas, either … or, neither … nor.

Examples:
a)   The boy **and** the girl hurried home.
b)   The dog was delighted with the bone **and** wagged his tail.
c)   **Both** he **and** his wife went on holiday.
d)   **Both** the driver **and** the man, who was hurt, were questioned.
e)   He was poor **but** honest.
f)   She could write well, **but** she could not do her sums.
g)   I gave him the money, **for** he had earned it.
h)   I am surprised at him **for** he should know better.
i)   He worked hard, **whereas** I did very little.
j)   He thought himself wealthy, **whereas** he was poor.
k)   **Either** my brother **or** his chum knows the place.
l)   **Either** my nephew goes with me **or** he stays at home.
m)   **Neither** James **nor** Mary wants to go.
n)   **Neither** did he come **nor** did he send any excuse.

2. Conjunctions which join principal clauses to subordinate clauses.
(Included are many adverbs which act as connecting words and therefore become conjunctions.) In order to distinguish the various types of conjunction in this class they are grouped under the appropriate headings below:

Time

Conjunctions are:

after, before, since, until, till, when, whenever, while, now, that, as.

Examples:
a)   **After** the lady opened the door she switched on the light.
b)   The man ate a sandwich **before** he boarded the bus.
c)   **Since** I have known her we have been firm friends.

d) We will wait here **until** the next train arrives.

e) I cannot say definitely **till** I hear from him.

f) The boys were going to school **when** we saw them.

g) **Whenever** it is possible we shall visit her.

h) **While** there is life there is hope.

i) **Now that** we have finished, let us go home.

j) **As** I was on my way home, I fell.

Place

Conjunctions are:

whence, where, wherever, whither.

Examples:

a) He looked back **whence** he had come.

b) Put it **where** he cannot see it.

c) The brooch must be found **wherever** it is.

d) **Whither** thou goest, I will go.

Cause or Reason

Conjunctions are:

as, because, lest, since.

Examples:

a) **As** he was in a hurry I did not speak to him.

b) We know he was to blame **because** we saw the accident.

c) I was afraid **lest** he should fall.

d) Do not say anything **since** she is frightened.

Concession

Conjunctions are:

although, even if, though, whether ... or, while, as.

Examples:

a) **Although** I have written twice, he has not replied.

b) I would not go **even if** I were invited.

c) **Though** the boy had faults I could not but like him.

d) It is the truth **whether** you believe it **or** not.

e) **While** we should condemn vice, we should praise virtue.

f) He could not get the answer, clever **as** he was.

Condition

Conjunctions are:

except that, if, unless.

Examples:
a)   **Except that** she is a trifle slow, she writes well.
b)   Send me word **if** you wish to go.
c)   That rascal will do nothing **unless** he is compelled.

Manner or Degree

Conjunctions are:

as, as . . . as, as if, as though, so . . . as, than.

Examples:
a)   He remained at home **as** he had been ordered.
b)   The house is vacant **as** far **as** we know.
c)   He speaks **as if** he knows all about it.
d)   The animal lay **as though** it were dead.
e)   James does not read **so** well **as** Robert.
f)   He is taller **than** I am.

Purpose

Conjunctions are:

in order that, lest, so that, that.

Examples:
a)   They worked hard **in order that** they might finish in time.
b)   Take care, **lest** you are hurt.
c)   I sent him a letter **so that** he would know.
d)   You come to school **that** you may learn.

Consequence

Conjunctions are:

so that, so .... that.

Examples:
a)   The man spoke loudly **so that** he was easily heard.
b)   She is **so** dull **that** she can learn nothing.

Exercises on Conjunctions

In the following exercises there are sentences with groups of two words within brackets. One of the two words is correct, the other wrong. Underline the correct word:

Time
1. Wait there (how, till) I have finished.
2. He left (before, that) darkness fell.
3. We have remained here (whether, since) you left.
4. (After, Unless) they arrived, they sat down.
5. I can call (however, whenever) it is convenient to you.
6. The exercise will be corrected (before, when) it is finished.
7. His brother waited (except, until) James returned.
8. She read a book (that, while) I wrote a letter.
9. (Now that, Unless) the weather has changed the farmers can expect good crops.
10. (Until, As) he went up the stairs, he stumbled.

Place
1. He went (whence, unless) he could not return.
2. The faithful dog followed his master (lest, wherever) he went.
3. There were many trees (since, where) I sat down.
4. They followed (whither, than) he led them.

Cause or Reason
1. (As, Where) we left early, we did not see him.
2. I was afraid to speak (lest, however) he should tell.
3. You ask him, (since, than) you are friends.
4. My uncle was angry (where, because) he was deceived.

Concession
1. The boy is strong and healthy (though, since) he is not tall.
2. (While, Unless) I trust him, I dislike his companions.
3. We will go (how, even if) it rains.
4. (Whether, Where) you like it or not, he will invite you.
5. My cold is much worse (although, whence) I have tried to cure it.

Exercises   on Conjunctions continued

Condition
1. (Except that, Unless) he is sometimes nervous, he manages quite well.
2. She will go (than, if) you ask her.
3. You cannot obtain admission (unless, since) you pay.

Manner or Degree
1. You are quite right (while, as far as) I can see.
2. The dog lifted his paw (as though, how) he understood me.
3. She is older (than, since) I am.
4. They did not play (while, so well as) their opponents.
5. The man looked (when, as if) he was a foreigner.
6. I cannot work (as, whence) he can.

Purpose
1. The man put on the light (so that, since) he could read.
2. (In order that, When) they might be in time, they left early.
3. The boy ran quickly (why, lest) he should be left behind.
4. You should go (that, how) you may be cured.

Consquence
1. The dog ran so fast (that, while) he caught the hare.
2. He ran quickly (when, so that) he was in time for tea.

Prepositions

The Preposition is placed before (pre) a noun or a pronoun. It defines a relationship to the noun or pronoun.

The following list contains the most common prepositions:

about, above, across, after, against, along, amid, amidst, among, amongst, around, at, before, behind, below, beneath, beside, between, betwixt, beyond, by, down, during, except, for, from, in, into, near, of, off, on, over, round, since, through, till, to, towards, under, underneath, until, unto, up, upon, with, within, without.

Exercises   on Prepositions

1. **Use the correct prepositions in the blank spaces:**
   a) The boy must apologise __to__ the lady.
   b) That man is an authority __for__ flowers.
   c) The mother was proud __of__ her son's success.
   d) He placed the bat __on__ the wall.
   e) My cousin put the book __into__ the drawer.
   f) It is an exception __above__ the rule.
   g) His opinion differs __from__ mine.
   h) The man ran __by__ the path.
   i) She takes great pride __about__ her appearance.
   j) The ball went __through__ the window.

2. **Supply three suitable prepositions in each sentence:**

   a) The pencil lay { __on__ / __upon__ / __across__ } the desk.

   b) The man rowed { __across__ / __along__ / __among__ } the river.

   c) The lady sat { __with__ / __near__ / __along__ } the chairman.

3. **Underline the prepositions in the following sentences:**
   a) I stood on the <u>bridge</u> of the ship.
   b) Above me, I saw a <u>cloudy</u> sky.
   c) The dog <u>leaped</u> over the wall after a ball.
   d) We chased him <u>through</u> a field of hay.
   e) With that ticket you can <u>obtain</u> admission to the show.
   f) My brother <u>received</u> a letter from him.

90

Exercises on Prepositions continued

g) The farmer stored his hay in a large barn.

h) Beside the boxes lay several boulders.

i) The careless boy ran behind the car.

j) During the year many people were injured in street accidents.

Many people find it difficult to choose the correct prepositions. The following should be read carefully and revised from time to time:

according to	good for
afflict with	guilty of
agree to (something)	in defiance of
agree with (somebody)	indignant at (something)
aim at	indignant with (somebody)
angry at (something)	inspired by
angry with (somebody)	interfere with
ashamed of	invasion of
blame for	meddle with
change for (something)	mount an attack on
change with (somebody)	opposite to
comment on	part from (somebody)
compared with	part with (something)
complain of	prevail on
confer with	protest against
conscious of	pursuit of
despair of	recoil from
die of	regard for
differ from (opinion)	rely on
differ with (somebody)	similar to
disagree with	suffer from
disappointed in (something)	tired of (something)
disappointed with (somebody)	tired with (action)
disgusted at (something)	thirst for (or after)
disgusted with (somebody)	vexed at (something)
dislike for	vexed with (somebody)
divide among (many)	victim of
divide between (two)	wait for (person, thing)
equal to	wait upon (somebody)
filled with	write about (something)
full of	write to (somebody)

Correction of Sentences

There are errors in the following sentences. Rewrite them correctly.

1. She was the oldest of the two sisters.
2. Who did you see at the party?
3. Neither John or James were present.
4. She is not as old as me.
5. The best team won the football match.
6. The books what we read were interesting.
7. Being a fine day I went to the seashore.
8. Who can it be for?
9. He was angry at me for leaving.
10. I am your's truly.
11. I cannot run no farther.
12. John has broke his leg.
13. Hurrah shouted the man.
14. The letter was sent to Mr Jane Brown.
15. The parcel was returned back to the sender.
16. I left home at quarter to 7.
17. The girl said that she done it herself.
18. He returned home as quick as he could.
19. I have forgot to post the letter.
20. "Where is my Boots?"
21. She hurted her leg.
22. She got a bad accident.
23. There is four books on the table.
24. He went for to get up.
25. The lady bought a comb for the baby with plastic teeth.
26. Between you and I he is quite wrong.
27. They sung the same song twice.
28. This jacket is wore out.
29. It's no use me working.
30. I intended to have written.
31. I was that tired I could hardly of spoken.
32. The fishermen saw a flock of herring in the sea.
33. Immediately he ran to the injured man.
34. Between you and me we seen many people.
35. I saw a dog with his master which had a long tail.
36. We found the ring belonging to the lady made of gold.
37. A piano was sold to a lady with carved legs.
38. We seen the rascal who stole were ball.
39. There is five books on the table.

92

40. A man was at the corner and his dog. *(with)*
41. She and her husband am going. *(are)*
42. His hair needs cutting badly. *(badly)*
43. Neither of them are tall.
44. Someone's left their books behind. *(has)*
45. Him and his sister went to the cinema. *(He)*
46. Me and my friend went to buy a coat for ourselves. *(we) (us)*
47. It was him you saw.
48. They have did it again. *(done)*
49. She could not come no quicker. *(any)*
50. We have never seen none of them. *(any)*
51. He couldn't remember nothing. *(anything)*
52. He done his work correctly. *(did)*
53. Is he the tallest of the two?
54. Each of the boys had their books. *(his)*
55. It was me that broke the window. *(I)*
56. Which is the cleverest, John or Mary? *(who) (cleverer)*
57. A more kinder man never lived.
58. I was that breathless I could hardly speak. *(so)*
59. The animal did not take no notice. *(any)*
60. Neither of them have been lucky. *(has)*
61. Me and him went together to the cinema. *(He) (I)*
62. He took the biggest half. *(bigger)*
63. It was a remarkable fine picture. *(remarkably)*
64. He is worse than me. *(I)*
65. I seen him go to the theatre. *(saw)*
66. One of the horses were tired. *(was)*
67. Of the two, I like James best. *(better)*
68. Give me them oranges. *(those)*
69. He don't speak very clear. *(doesn't)*
70. We are quite sure he done it. *(did)*
71. She sent it to you and I. *(me)*
72. The man learnt him to swim. *(taught)*
73. That answer is different with mine. *(from)*
74. Neither one or the other is right.
75. She will not stay, I do not think.
76. The lady sings quite nice. *(nicely)*
77. He did not except the gift. *(accept)*
78. To who does this belong?
79. The child rose up from the floor.
80. The two brothers divided the apple among them. *(shared)*

The Right Word in the Right Place

1. Place the following words in the sentences best suited to their use:

closed, finished, stopped, completed, concluded, ended.

   a) His watch *stopped* at six o'clock.
   b) I remember how the story *ended*.
   c) I have *finished* my lessons.
   d) They have *completed* the alterations.
   e) The meeting *concluded* with the National Anthem.
   f) Having enough money, they *closed* the fund.

2. Explain the difference between:

learning – teaching, looking – staring, mumbling – bawling,
striding – galloping, taking – snatching, tapping – battering,
throwing – hurling, writing – scribbling.

3. Use the following words (instead of "nice") to describe:

agreeable, beautiful, convenient, delicious, enjoyable, fine, good, interesting, pleasant, pretty.

a *beautiful* garden   a *pretty* bonnet
a *delicious* cake   a *pleasant* walk
a *good* house   an *agreeable* man
a *fine* day   a *convenient* train
an *enjoyable* concert   an *interesting* book

4. Place the following words in the sentences best suited to them:

frowned, mumbled, sang, chuckled, bowed, whispered, listened, smiled.

He *sang* tunefully.   He *chuckled* gleefully.
He *frowned* angrily.   He *smiled* broadly.
He *bowed* humbly.   He *listened* attentively.
He *mumbled* indistinctly.   He *whispered* softly.

5. Place the following words in the sentences best suited to their use:

exclaimed, muttered, answered, said, shouted, explained, whispered, pleaded.

He *pleaded* that he would come.   He *exclaimed* with joy.
He *explained* why he was late.   "Look!" he *said*.
He *shouted* for mercy.   He *muttered* under his breath.
He *whispered* quietly to his   "That is so," he *answered*
neighbour.

6. Place the following words in the sentences best suited to them:

caressed, ate, pulled, charged, slept, bled, crept, strove.

He _charged_ furiously.   He _ate_ greedily.

He _____ profusely.   He _slept_ soundly.

He _pulled_ vigorously.   He _____ manfully.

He _____ fondly.   He _crept_ stealthily.

7. Always avoid use of the word "got". There is usually another word which can be used to better effect.

Substitute a better word in each of the following sentences:

a) He **got up** at eight o'clock.

b) He **got** a penny from his mother.

c) He **got** his breakfast early.

d) He **got** a bad cold yesterday.

e) He **got to** the station in time.

f) He **got** married last year.

8. Write in the most suitable word:

a) A man who digs for coal is a _miner_.

b) I switched on the _dim_ light.

c) The _Christmas_ holiday is in December.

d) They sang a Christmas _carol_.

e) He was so ill _that_ he went to bed.

f) The postman _posted_ the letters.

g) He avoided accidents because he drove very _cautiously_

9. Place the right words (from **who**, **whom**, **whose**, **which**) in the following sentences:

a) That is the boy _who_ broke the window.

b) That is the stone _which_ broke the window.

c) That is the man _whose_ window was broken.

d) That is the boy _whom_ I saw breaking the window.

e) That is the boy _who_ told me that he broke the window.

10. Words ending in "-able":

a) A piece of furniture. _table_

b) A horse's home. _stable_

c) Written by Æsop.

d) Can be carried. _portable_

e) Diamonds are. _collectable_

f) A telegram from overseas.

g) Helpless.

h) Land under cultivation.

i) A carrot. _vegetable_

j) Glass things are. _breakable_

11. Give a single word for each of the following:

a) go away, *leave*   b) go back, *return*   c) go down, *descend*   d) go forward, *advance*

e) go into, *enter*   f) go on hands and knees, *crawl*   g) go out of, *exit*   h) go quickly, *fast*

i) go slowly, *scantily*   j) go up. *ascend*

12. Place the right words (from **no**, **not**, **never**, **none**, **any**) in the following sentences:

a) Did you notice _any_ friends there?

b) _Never_ have I seen such a display.

c) We have _not_ received _any_ of the books.

d) _No_ thank you, I _never_ smoke.

e) We are _not_ going there _any_ more.

f) _None_ of the boys knew the answer.

g) _No_, he is _not_ well enough to eat _any_ cakes.

h) Have you _any_ marbles? _No_, I have _none_.

13. From the following lengths choose the correct one for each sentence:

two millimetres; fifteen centimetres; thirty centimetres; one hundred and eighty centimetres; four metres; seventy metres; six hundred and forty-three kilometres; four thousand eight hundred and twenty-seven kilometres.

a) The soldier was _4 m_ tall.

b) My exercise book is _15 cm_ wide.

c) The height of the factory chimney was _70 m_.

d) The distance from London to Glasgow is about _643 km_.

e) The string on the parcel was _2 mm_ thick.

f) The distance from Southampton to New York is about _4827 km_.

g) The room was _4 m_ high.

h) My ruler is _30 cm_ long.

14. Explain the difference between:

yacht – steamer,   car – aeroplane,   river – canal,

pen – pencil,   shoes – boots,   chair – sofa,

pin – needle,   ham – bacon,   shadow – reflection,

clock – watch,   saltfish – cod,   hay – straw,

cigar – cheroot,   picture – sketch,   map – plan,

ceiling – roof.

15. There are a great many words to describe different ways of walking. For example: A hunter **walked** over the hills. A better word here would be **roved** or **roamed**.

In the sentences below replace the word **walked** by a more suitable word from the following list. Any word once used may not be used again, so be careful and **watch your step:**

limped, strode, sneaked, toddled, paced, rambled, tramped, shuffled, plodded, strutted, strolled, stamped, hobbled, marched, sauntered, prowled.

a)   The nature lover **walked** through the woods.   *sauntered*
b)   The lame man **walked** across the floor.   *plodded*
c)   The happy couple **walked** down the lane.   *strutted*   *shuffled*
d)   The daring knight **walked** into the hall.   *shuffled*   *strode*
e)   The tourist **walked** through the art gallery.   *prowled*
f)   The soldiers **walked** to the station.   *marched*
g)   Captain Smith **walked** up and down the deck.   *paced*
h)   The cunning thief **walked** into the room.   *strolled*
i)   The baby **walked** across the floor.   *toddled*
j)   Proud Mr Brown **walked** on to the platform.   *rambled*
k)   The weary farmer **walked** homewards.   *limped*
l)   A gouty old man **walked** down the stairs.   *tramped*
m)   The hikers **walked** many a long mile.   *strode*
n)   The angry man **walked** into his office.   *stamped*
o)   The burglar **walked** through the house.   *sneaked*
p)   The sick patient **walked** over to the table.   *hobbled*

16. The following may be said to be **the right action at the right time**. Tell what immediate action you would take and suggest a cure (if necessary). What would you do?

a)   If you burned your foot.   *pour water on it*
b)   If you lost your way.   *ask an adult*
c)   If you sprained your ankle.   *put ice on it*
d)   If your nose started to bleed.   *hold your nose and tilt your head backwards*
e)   If you noticed an escape of gas in the house.   *call 999*
f)   If your sister's dress caught fire.   *pour water on it (then buy her a new one.)*
g)   If you found a wallet in the street.   *give it to a policeman*
h)   If your brother's hand was cut.   *get a plaster*
i)   If you saw smoke coming from a closed shop.   *call the police*
j)   If your cousin was stung in the arm.   *get a plaster*

Addition of Clauses

Add a clause to the following and name the kind of clause you add:

1. I saw the lady _eating_ . _Verb_
2. The little boy said _I am lost_ . _Verb_
3. The girl ran quickly _towards home_ . _Verb_
4. _Rushing Banging_ _Verb_ when they reached home.
5. I noticed _he was struggling_ _Verb_ when he rose to speak.
6. We stood on the very spot _of the cliff naing_ _Verb_ .
7. _Drowning will happen_ _Verb_ if you cannot swim.
8. The dog barked loudly _at the tree_ _Noun_ .
9. The lady _stared at whom_ _Verb_ was my sister.
10. "Will you let me know _where the party is_ _Noun_ ?"
11. The dog _heroicly_ _Verb_ saved the child.
12. We saw the train _go pass_ _Verb_ .
13. I hope _she goes nee_ _Verb_ .
14. _I spoke_ _Verb_ while they listened.
15. The boy hurt himself badly _running_ _Verb_ .
16. The man _ran as he_ _Verb_ was caught by the police.
17. I saw _the fish swimming_ _Verb_ .
18. She bought an umbrella _because it was raining_ _Verb_ .
19. _____ as she spoke.
20. The messenger arrived _____.
21. I watched the man _____
22. I do not know _____.
23. As the girl approached the house _____
24. We saw_____ when we returned.
25. _____ if you are ill.
26. "Come to my house _____"
27. I know the child _____
28. When I came here _____.
29. _____ which cost two pence.
30. My father scolded me _____
31. The crowd rushed forward _____.
32. The soldiers_____ were trapped in the wood.
33. The unhappy scholar said _____
34. _____ if you do not send word.
35. The boy lifted the box _____.
36. The man waved frantically _____

Replacement

Change the underlined phrases into clauses:

1. He failed <u>through carelessness</u>.
2. <u>On the completion of his task</u> the boy went out to play.
3. He told me <u>of his coming</u>.
4. A man <u>in high position</u> has many responsibilities.
5. She lived in a cottage <u>near the sea</u>.
6. <u>On entering</u> I saw several pictures.
7. The police recovered <u>the stolen property</u>.
8. I was pleased to hear <u>of his success</u>.
9. We do not know <u>his hiding place</u>.
10. The roads <u>leading to the fair</u> were crowded.

Change the underlined clauses into phrases:

1. I am convinced <u>that he is sincere</u>.
2. The child was in bed <u>before the sun had set</u>.
3. His action showed <u>how brave he was</u>.
4. I am certain <u>that you will help me</u>.
5. <u>As I approached</u> I heard a great noise.
6. He met me <u>when I arrived</u>.
7. The man admitted <u>that he was wrong</u>.
8. The girl was absent <u>because she was ill</u>.
9. You cannot succeed <u>unless you work hard</u>.
10. The witness described <u>where the accident took place</u>.

Replace the words underlined by a single word:

1. He wished to see him <u>at once</u>.
2. The concert was <u>put off</u> for a month.
3. The sentry <u>ran away</u> from his post.
4. The concert is held <u>once every year</u>.
5. The army <u>went forward</u> towards the town.
6. The man <u>was sorry</u> for his hasty words.
7. The sun <u>went out of sight</u> behind the clouds.
8. The <u>people who live next door</u> are very kind.
9. They <u>made up their minds</u> to go to the party.
10. That boy is always <u>in time</u>.

Sentences

Simple to Complex

Make each pair of simple sentences into one complex sentence and retain the meaning as far as possible.

(Do not use "and" or "but" or "so".)

1. a) I have a dog. b) I am very fond of it.
2. a) That is the man. b) He stole my purse.
3. a) I was travelling in a bus. b) It collided with a taxi.
4. a) The boy did not pass. b) His work was badly done.
5. a) I was gazing out of the window. b) I saw a crowd.
6. a) The boy was riding a horse. b) It looked tired.
7. a) The man could hardly walk. b) He carried such a heavy load.
8. a) The book belongs to Jack. b) It is a red one.
9. a) The girl went for the doctor. b) The doctor stayed next door.
10. a) The house was destroyed. b) It was built by Tom's father.
11. a) He works hard at his lessons. b) He wishes to succeed.
12. a) The men were walking quickly. b) The men saw me.
13. a) He heard the sound of music. b) He was passing a church.
14. a) The lady lost the book. b) She was going to the library.
15. a) The man stood at the door. b) The door was open.
16. a) The boy caught a rabbit. b) He took it home.
17. a) The girl fell heavily. b) The girl hurt herself.
18. a) He opened the cupboard. b) He saw many books.
19. a) The lady was careless. b) She lost her purse.
20. a) Mary entered the room. b) The room was brightly decorated.
21. a) A loud peal of thunder came. b) The children were frightened.
22. a) Tom made mistakes in reading. b) He could not see well.
23. a) The teacher praised the boys. b) They had worked well.
24. a) The horse fell. b) It was pulling a heavy load.
25. a) The man caught a salmon. b) He took it home.

26. a) The boy has hurt his foot.   b) The boy cannot walk.
27. a) The lady sat in a coach.   b) Four horses drew it.
28. a) The tourist climbed the hill.   b) The hill was steep.
29. a) My sister has a good voice.   b) She sings in the choir.
30. a) The girl found a brooch.   b) She took it to her mother.
31. a) I found a lady's purse.   b) It contained two coins.
32. a) The girl wore a red dress.   b) She sat next to me.
33. a) I visited the little cottage.   b) I was born in it.
34. a) The woman was selling flowers.   b) She stood at the corner of the street.
35. a) I went to see my cousin.   b) His home was in the country.
36. a) The man was poorly clad.   b) I gave him money.

Complex to Simple

Change the following complex sentences into simple sentences and retain the meaning as far as possible:

1. He is a man who is very intelligent.
2. We heard the news that he was saved.
3. I can tell you how old he is.
4. The woman lives in a house which is very big.
5. Maria spoke to the soldier who was wounded.
6. The boy lost his ticket because he was careless.
7. I shall speak to him when he arrives.
8. The child found a ring which was very valuable.
9. He asked me where I lived.
10. Can you tell me which way the wind is blowing?
11. I saw him when the clock struck five.
12. We all believed the story that the traveller told.
13. Huge telescopes are used by people who study the stars.
14. As soon as the sun rose the soldiers resumed their march.
15. He asked for the book in which one finds the meanings of words.
16. I admit that I have made a mistake.

Alphabetical Order

The Alphabet (twenty-six letters)

A B C D E F G H I J K L M
N O P Q R S T U V W X Y Z

Practically all books containing lists have the words arranged in the order of the letters of the alphabet:

1. By the **first** letters of the words.
2. When the first letters are the same, the words are arranged according to the **second** letters.
3. When the first two letters are the same, the words are arranged according to the **third** letters.
   And so on.

Examples:

1. **By the first letter:**

   anchor, bicycle, height, machine, physical, seized, vehicle, yacht.

2. **When the first letters are the same:**

   absence, accurate, aeroplane, ancient, attention, autumn, awkward.

3. **When the first two letters are the same:**

   thatch, their, thimble, though, through, thumb, thyme.

Exercises on Alphabetical Order

1. Place the following words in alphabetical order:

   colonel, extremely, immediately, judgement, language, necessary, official, vegetable

   vegetable, official, judgement, colonel, extremely, necessary, language, immediately.

2. Rearrange the following words in dictionary order:

   balance, beginning, biscuit, blossom, bough, brooch, business, byre

   beginning, brooch, biscuit, business, byre, bough, balance, blossom.

3. Place the following words in alphabetical order:

   complaint, cocoa, correct, coffee, condition, coarse, collection, course.

4. Rearrange the following words in dictionary order:

   dismissed, disguise, displayed, disaster, district, discovery, disobeyed, disease.

Apostrophes

The Possessive Case of a Noun is shown by a mark (') known as an apostrophe.

In **Singular** nouns it is shown by **'s**, e.g. Mary's bag, the animal's foot, Keats's poems, Burns's songs. *Exception*: it may however be shown by the **apostrophe only** (') to avoid awkward-sounding double or treble s endings, e.g. Moses' anger, Jesus' words, Aristophanes' comedies.

In the **Plural** it is shown in **two** ways:

a) **By the apostrophe only** (') when the plural ends in **-s** or **-es**, e.g. the boys' books, the ladies' coats.

b) **By the apostrophe and s** (**'s**) when the **plural does not end in s**, e.g. the children's toys, the men's hats.

Singular Possessive	**Plural Possessive**
the girl's dress	the girls' dresses
the lady's bag	the ladies' bags
the boy's pencil	the boys' pencils
a day's work	seven days' work
the man's pipe	the men's pipes
the woman's glove	the women's gloves
the child's clothes	the children's clothes

Exercises   on Apostrophes

Correct the following sentences by putting in the apostrophes:

1. The boys pencil lay on the floor.
2. The ladies coats were in the cloakroom.
3. My cousins hand was badly hurt.
4. The mens boots were covered with mud.
5. The childs doll fell into the pond.
6. I saw that the object was a womans glove.
7. The register lay on the teachers desk.
8. He looked very smart in page-boys uniform.
9. It took several hours hard work to repair the damage.
10. In the window was a special display of babies clothes.
11. The childrens books were left in my uncles house.
12. The maids dress was torn by a neighbours dog.
13. My fathers wallet was discovered in the thieves den.
14. A ducks egg is generally cheaper than a hens.
15. Mr Smiths watch is five minutes slower than Mr Browns.

The Apostrophe as a Contraction

When the apostrophe is used to contract words it is placed where the letters have been omitted, e.g.

all's	all is	o'clock	of the clock
can't	cannot	o'er	over
couldn't	could not	shan't	shall not
'cross	across	she'll	she will
didn't	did not	shouldn't	should not
doesn't	does not	that's	that is
don't	do not	there's	there is
hasn't	has not	they'll	they will
haven't	have not	we'll	we will
he'd	he would	we've	we have
he'll	he will	whate'er	whatever
he's	he is	where'er	wherever
I'll	I will	whosoe'er	whosoever
I'd	I would	who've	who have
I'm	I am	won't	will not
isn't	is not	wouldn't	would not
it's	it is	you'll	you will
I've	I have	you're	you are

Exercises   on the Apostrophe as a Contraction

1. **Insert the apostrophe where it should be:**

    tis, neednt, youll, Halloween, souwester, Ive, twas, neer, oclock, dont.

2. **Write the following sentence making use of the apostrophe as a contraction:**

    We will probably arrive at seven of the clock if there is a convenient bus.

Capital Letters

Capital letters are used:

1. to begin sentences
2. to begin special names
3. to begin direct speech
4. to begin words in titles
5. to begin lines of poetry
6. to begin words of exclamation
7. to begin words He, Him, His, if they refer to God or Christ
8. to write the word "I".

1. Beginning Sentences

One day a girl was playing on a busy street. Her ball rolled into the middle of the road and she ran after it. At that moment a car came dashing round the corner. A passer-by saw the girl's danger and ran quickly to her aid. Fortunately he saved her from serious injury.

2. Special Names

Jean Miller and her brother David are expected to arrive by Concorde from New York on Tuesday, November 30th, St Andrew's Day.

3. Direct Speech

A man said to his friends, "If you manage to solve the puzzle, send me the answer." His companions replied, "We will send you our solution before the end of the week."

4. Titles

The famous collection of Indian animal stories called *The Jungle Book* was written by Rudyard Kipling.

5. Lines of Poetry

I wandered lonely as a cloud
    That floats on high o'er vales and hills,
When all at once I saw a crowd,
    A host of golden daffodils,
Beside the lake, beneath the trees,
Fluttering and dancing in the breeze.

6. Exclamation

"Oh!" shouted the boy, "I have hurt my finger." "Indeed!" exclaimed his father, "You are lucky to get off so lightly."

7. Reference to God or Christ

   After Jesus had preached to the multitude He proceeded on His way to Jerusalem.

8. The Pronoun "I"

   He advised me to travel by bus but I told him that I preferred to travel by rail.

Punctuation

By correct punctuation we mean the proper use of:

   capital letters, comma (,), full stop or period (.), quotation marks (" "),
   exclamation mark (!), question mark (?) and apostrophe (').

Punctuate the following sentences:

1. What time is it asked the traveller
2. His father said where is your brothers knife
3. My friend exclaimed what a lovely view
4. He has gone to school said his sister in a quiet voice
5. The child suddenly shouted look
6. Oh cried the boy i have hurt my finger
7. Come here said his mother all right replied the boy
8. The man asked have you seen the hammer yes replied his companion it is on the table
9. A boy said to his friend are you going to the cinema no replied the other im on my way home
10. When i return said the girl to her father will you tell me the story of the shipwreck very well he answered but dont be too long at your aunts

Diminutives

booklet	cygnet	cigarette	laddie	chicken
bracelet	eaglet	epaulette	lassie	kitten
goblet	islet	kitchenette	bullock	maiden
leaflet	leveret	pipette	hillock	cubicle
ringlet	locket	rosette	damsel	icicle
rivulet	owlet	statuette	morsel	particle
baronet	pocket	duckling	satchel	lambkin
circlet	darling	nestling	gosling	mannikin
sapling	seedling	dearie	globule	napkin
coronet	briquette	girlie	molecule	piglet

Small Quantities

air	· a breath, puff, whiff	paper	· a scrap
bread	· a crumb, crust, morsel	rain	· a drop, spot
butter	· a pat, nut	salt	· a grain, pinch
colour	· a dab, tint, touch	sand	· a grain, particle
corn	· an ear	smoke	· a wisp
dirt	· a particle, speck, spot	snuff	· a pinch
energy	· an ounce	soot	· a smut, speck
flowers	· a nosegay, posy	straw	· a wisp
food	· a morsel, particle, scrap	sugar	· a grain, spoonful
glass	· a splinter, fragment	tea	· a pinch, spoonful
grass	· a blade, tuft	time	· a moment, second
hair	· a lock, strand	water	· a drop, sip
light	· a beam, glimmer, ray	wind	· a puff, whiff
liquid	· a drop, sip	wood	· a chip, splinter

For Reference

To Find / **Look at**

1. the address of a person — directory
2. the meaning of a word — dictionary
3. the day and date of the month — calendar
4. the position of a place — atlas
5. a list of priced goods or books — catalogue
6. a telephone number — telephone directory
7. the time of a train or bus — timetable
8. record of a ship's progress at sea — log
9. record of attendance — register
10. record of personal daily events — diary
11. collection of photos and autographs — album
12. extracts from books and papers — scrapbook
13. record of recent happenings — newspaper
14. facts regarding days of the year — almanac
15. a fictitious tale — novel
16. a life story — biography
17. material regarding living creatures — book on zoology
18. material regarding plants — book on botany
19. material regarding the stars — book on astronomy
20. material regarding the Earth's crust — book on geology

Proverbs

Proverbs are popular sayings expressed in a clever, brief manner.

1. A bad workman always blames his tools.
2. Absence makes the heart grow fonder.
3. A bird in the hand is worth two in the bush.
4. A cat may look at a king.
5. A drowning man will clutch at a straw.
6. A fool and his money are soon parted.
7. A friend in need is a friend indeed.
8. A hungry man is an angry man.
9. All's well that ends well.
10. An apple a day keeps the doctor away.
11. A miss is as good as a mile.
12. A penny saved is a penny gained.
13. A rolling stone gathers no moss.
14. A stitch in time saves nine.
15. As well be hanged for a sheep as a lamb.
16. A small leak will sink a great ship.
17. As the twig is bent so the tree's inclined.
18. As you make your bed so must you lie in it.
19. Better late than never.
20. Birds of a feather flock together.
21. Charity begins at home.
22. Cut your coat according to your cloth.
23. Discretion is the better part of valour.
24. Don't carry all your eggs in one basket.
25. Don't count your chickens before they are hatched.
26. Early to bed, early to rise, makes a man healthy, wealthy and wise.
27. Empty vessels make most noise.
28. Enough is as good as a feast.
29. Every cloud has a silver lining.
30. Every dog has its day.
31. Faint heart never won fair lady.
32. Fair exchange is no robbery.
33. Fine feathers make fine birds.
34. Fine words butter no parsnips.

35. Fire is a good servant but a bad master.

36. First come, first served.

37. Forbidden fruit tastes sweetest.

38. Good wine needs no bush.

39. Great minds think alike.

40. Great oaks from little acorns grow.

41. Habit is second nature.

42. Half a loaf is better than no bread.

43. He laughs best who laughs last.

44. He who pays the piper calls the tune.

45. Hunger is the best sauce.

46. Imitation is the sincerest form of flattery.

47. In for a penny, in for a pound.

48. It's a long lane that has no turning.

49. It's an ill wind that blows nobody any good.

50. Laugh and grow fat.

51. Least said, soonest mended.

52. Leave well alone.

53. Let not the pot call the kettle black.

54. Let sleeping dogs lie.

55. Listeners hear no good of themselves.

56. Children should be seen and not heard.

57. Look after the pence, and the pounds will look after themselves.

58. Look before you leap.

59. Love laughs at locksmiths.

60. Make hay while the sun shines.

61. Misery makes strange bedfellows.

62. More haste, less speed.

63. Necessity is the mother of invention.

64. New brooms sweep clean.

65. None but the brave deserve the fair.

66. None so deaf as those who will not hear.

67. No news is good news.

68. No smoke without fire.

69. Once bitten twice shy.

70. One good turn deserves another.

71. One man's meat is another man's poison.
72. One swallow does not make a summer.
73. Out of sight, out of mind.
74. Out of the frying pan into the fire.
75. Penny wise, pound foolish.
76. Pride goes before a fall.
77. Robbing Peter to pay Paul.
78. Sauce for the goose is sauce for the gander.
79. Set a thief to catch a thief.
80. Silence gives consent.
81. Spare the rod and spoil the child.
82. Speech is silvern, silence is golden.
83. Still waters run deep.
84. The early bird catches the worm.
85. Too many cooks spoil the broth.
86. Truth will out.
87. Two heads are better than one.
88. Unity is strength.
89. We never miss the water till the well runs dry.
90. Where there's a will there's a way.
91. When the cat's away the mice will play.

Colloquialisms

Colloquialisms are expressions used in common conversation.

the apple of one's eye	somebody specially dear
armed to the teeth	completely armed
a wet blanket	a discouraging person
dead beat	exhausted
in the same boat	in the same circumstances
carried away	highly excited
a chip off the old block	very like one's father or mother
under a cloud	in trouble or disfavour
down in the mouth	in low spirits
down on one's luck	in ill-luck
all ears	paying close attention
at a loose end	having nothing to do
off form	not so capable as usual
good for nothing	useless
a son of a gun	a likeable rogue
hard of hearing	almost deaf
hard up	short of money
hard hit	seriously troubled
ill-used	badly treated
lion-hearted	of great courage
at loggerheads	quarrelling
the man in the street	an ordinary man
up to the mark	good enough, well enough
an old salt	an experienced sailor
a peppery individual	a cranky, hot-tempered person
a pocket Hercules	a small but strong man
at rest	dead
a rough diamond	a person of real worth but rough manners
silver-tongued	plausible and eloquent
golden-voiced	pleasing to hear
out of sorts	not well
on the level	honest
stuck up	conceited
thick in the head	stupid
beside oneself	out of one's mind (with anger, grief)
heavy-eyed	sleepy

General Colloquial Expressions

to	to
weigh anchor	lift the anchor
keep up appearances	maintain an outward show
have a bee in one's bonnet	be obsessed with an idea
put one's best foot forward	do best possible
sweep the board	take all
make no bones about it	be plain and outspoken
burn the candle at both ends	overdo work and play
have one's heart in one's boots	be very despondent
have one's heart in one's mouth	be frightened
bury the hatchet	make peace
make a clean breast of	confess
have a feather in one's cap	have something to be proud of
set one's cap at	try to captivate
throw in the cards	give up the struggle
throw in the towel	give up the struggle
cast up	reproach
show a clean pair of heels	escape by running
pull up short	stop suddenly
wait till the clouds roll by	await more favourable circumstances
turn one's coat	change one's principles or allegiance
give the cold shoulder	show indifference or ignore
throw cold water on	discourage
cut a dash	be very showy
lead a dance	delude
lead up the garden path	deceive by hiding real intention
keep a thing dark	hide something
keep one's distance	stay aloof
lead a dog's life	have a wretched life
draw the line	fix the limit
keep one's powder dry	be ready or prepared
pull wool over the eyes	deceive
make both ends meet	manage financially
face the music	meet the worst
sit on the fence	avoid taking sides

to	to
put one's foot in it	cause embarrassment by word or action
fall foul of	come up against
get into hot water	get into trouble
take French leave	go without permission
play the game	act fairly
hit below the belt	act unfairly
hold one's tongue	keep silent
blow one's own trumpet	boast
hit the nail on the head	be right
bite the dust	fall to the ground, be defeated
kick over the traces	throw off control
knock on the head	stop suddenly
turn over a new leaf	conduct oneself better
pull someone's leg	hoax
tell it to the Marines	"no one believes that"
go through the mill	undergo suffering
put the cart before the horse	start at the wrong end
make the mouth water	cause to desire
sling mud	slander
nip in the bud	stop at an early stage
send someone packing	dismiss quickly
play fast and loose	act carelessly
keep the pot boiling	keep an activity going
rain cats and dogs	rain very heavily
raise one's dander	anger
mind your p's and q's	be careful about your behaviour
smell a rat	be suspicious
take a rise out of	fool
rub up the wrong way	irritate by opposing
get into hot water	get into trouble
turn the tables	reverse a result
back chat	be impudent
ride the high horse	be snobbish, arrogant
let the cat out of the bag	tell what should be kept secret
send to Coventry	ignore as a punishment
haul over the coals	scold or punish

to	to
take the bull by the horns	act despite risks
strike while the iron is hot	act without delay
take forty winks	sleep
chew the fat	argue
act the goat	behave foolishly
live from hand to mouth	live in hardship
hang one's head	feel ashamed
turn up one's nose	scorn deliberately
play with fire	tempt serious trouble
swing the lead	avoid work purposely
blaze the trail	lead the way
come a cropper	fail, fall to earth

Popular Phrases

Explain what is meant by the following phrases:

horse play
for a lark
a fine kettle of fish
as the crow flies
a stiff upper lip
a blind alley
a dead cert
a far cry
a flash in the pan
the lion's share
not a patch on
bats in the belfry
by hook or by crook

back to the wall
from pillar to post
a bird's eye view
a busman's holiday
no flies on him
a cat on hot bricks
a cock and bull story
with flying colours
a fly in the ointment
on the nail
pins and needles
a storm in a teacup

Doubles

Doubles are used in Speech to give greater emphasis.

1. By repetition of actual word:

again and again, by and by, neck and neck, out and out, over and over, round and round, so and so, such and such.

2. By repetition of meaning:

beck and call, ways and means, far and away, puff and blow, null and void, stuff and nonsense, fast and furious, odds and ends, rant and rave, lean and lanky, out and away, hue and cry, bawl and shout, old and grey.

3. By alliteration (words beginning with the same letter):

humming and hawing, kith and kin, might and main, part and parcel, safe and sound, hale and hearty, spick and span, alas and alack, time and tide, rack and ruin, rough and ready, one and only.

4. By opposites:

this and that, thick and thin, on and off, great and small, in and out, high and low, come and go, give and take, one and all, ups and downs, here and there.

5. By words of similar sound:

high and dry, fair and square, out and about, wear and tear.

6. By related words:

heart and soul, hip and thigh, tooth and nail, body and soul, root and branch, lock and key, hammer and tongs, hole and corner, head and shoulders, hand and foot.

7. Other examples:

all and sundry, fast and loose, fits and starts, hard and fast, free and easy, rough and tumble, habit and repute, over and above, touch and go, time and again.

Exercises on Doubles

Place the following phrases in the most suitable sentences:

again and again, lock and key, spick and span, puff and blow, odds and ends.

1. The police placed the man under _lock and key_.
2. He polished his boots until they were _spick and span_
3. She tried to do it _again and again_
4. The child had gathered many _odds and ends_
5. The stout man began to _puff and blow_ with exertion.

115

Colours

The following are the colours of the rainbow:
violet, indigo, blue, green, yellow, orange, red.

There are other colours, such as:
white, black, purple, brown, pink, grey, crimson.

Sometimes we refer to things as being:

blood-red,	bottle-green,	brick-red,	cinnamon-brown,	coal-black,
milk-white,	nut-brown,	pea-green,	primrose-yellow,	rose-pink,
ruby-red,	russet-brown,	sea-green,	shell-pink,	sky-blue,
slate-grey,	snow-white.			

Often we make use of "colour" words in everyday speech, e.g.

1. I saw it in **black and white**.
   I saw it in writing (or print).

2. I am in his **black books**.
   He is displeased with me.

3. The man **looked blue**.
   The man looked as if he was depressed in spirits.

4. He was in a **blue funk**.
   He was in great terror.

5. He had **blue blood** in his veins.
   He was of aristocratic descent.

6. The **green-eyed monster** caused him to strike his friend.
   Jealousy caused him to strike his friend.

7. He was a **greenhorn** at the game.
   He was raw and inexperienced at the game.

8. The fellow was **yellow at heart**.
   The fellow was really a coward.

9. He was born **in the purple**.
   He was of royal birth.

10. The business was a **white elephant**.
    The business was a failure.

11. It was a **red letter day** for me.
    It was a notable and fortunate day for me.

12. She **saw red** when she got the bill.
    She was very angry when she got the bill.

Exercises on Colours

Complete the following sentences:

1. The old colonel was purple with *rage*.
2. The bully turned white with *shock*.
3. The little child was blue with *a cold*.
4. His rival was green with *envy*.
5. The pages of the book were yellow with *age*.

Our Five Senses

Most people have five senses by which they are able to see, hear, smell, taste and touch.

Sight – is the ability to observe or perceive by the <u>eye</u>.

Hearing – is the ability to listen or perceive by the <u>ear</u>.

Smell – is the ability to detect odour or perceive by the <u>nose</u>.

Taste – is the ability to detect flavour in the mouth or perceive by the <u>tongue</u>.

Touch – is the ability to detect objects by contact or perceive by <u>feeling</u>.

Derivations

A **Root** is a word in its first and simplest form. A word may be built up or have its meaning changed by an addition at either end. The addition at the beginning is known as a **Prefix**, e.g. dis-agree. The addition at the end is known as a **Suffix**, e.g. paint-er.

Roots

Word	Meaning	Examples
aqua	water	aquatic, aqueduct
audio	I hear	audible, audience, audit
capio	I take	capable, captive, capture
centum	a hundred	centenarian, century
clamo	I shout	clamour, proclaim, exclaim
creo	create	creation, creature
curro	I run	courier, current, excursion

Word	Meaning	Examples
decem	ten	December, decimal
dico	I say	edict, dictation, verdict, dictator
duco	I lead	produce, reduce, introduce
facio	I make	fact, factory, perfect
finis	an end	final, infinite
fortis	strong	fort, fortify
homo	a man	homicide, human
impero	I command	empire, emperor, imperial
liber	free	liberal, liberty
malus	bad	malady, malice, maltreat
manus	hand	manual, manufacture, manuscript
mitto	I send	missile, mission, remittance
navis	a ship	navigate, navy
octo	eight	octagon, octave, October
pello	I drive	expel, propel, repel
pendeo	I hang	depend, pendant, suspend
pes	a foot	pedal, pedestrian, quadruped
planus	level	plain, plan, plane
plus	more	plural, surplus
porto	I carry	export, import, porter, transport
poto	I drink	poison, potion
primus	first	primer, primitive, Prime Minister
rego	I rule	regal, regent, regiment
rota	a wheel	rotate, rote, rotund
ruptus	broken	eruption, interruption, rupture
scribo	I write	scripture, describe, manuscript
specio	I see	aspect, prospect, spectacles
teneo	I hold	contain, retain, tentacles
unus	one	unit, unity, union
vanus	empty	vanish, vanity, vain
venio	I come	adventure, prevent, venture
video	I see	provident, visible, vision
vinco	I overcome	convince, victory
voco	I call	revoke, vocal, voice
volvo	I roll	evolve, revolve, volume

Prefixes

Prefix	Meaning	Examples
a-	on	afloat, ashore, aloft
a-, ab-, abs-	away, from	avert, absolve, abstract
ad-, ac-, ar- (etc.)	to	adhere, accept, arrive, assume, attract
ante-	before	antecedent, anteroom
anti-	against	antagonist, anti-aircraft
bi-, bis-	two, twice	bicycle, biped, bisect, biscuit
circum-	round	circumference, circuit
com-, con-	together	comparison, competition, contact
contra-	against	contrary, contraband, contradiction
de-	down	depress, descend, describe
dif-, dis-	apart, not	different, disagree, disappear
ex-	out of	exhale, export, extract
fore-	before	forecast, forenoon, foretell, foresee
im-, in-	in, into	import, include
in-	not	incapable, inhuman
inter-	between	international, interrupt, interval
mis-	wrong	misdeed, misjudge, mistake
ob-	against	object, obstruction
post-	after	postpone, postscript, post-war
pre-	before	predict, prepare, pre-war
pro-	forth	proceed, produce
re-	back	retake, return, retrace
sub-	under	submarine, subway
trans-	across	transfer, transport, transpose
un-	not, without	unfit, unknown, unpaid, unsafe
vice-	instead	vice-captain, viceroy

Suffixes

Suffix	Meaning	Examples
-able, -ible	capable of being	movable, edible, incredible
-ain, -an	one connected	chaplain, publican
-ance, -ence	state of	repentance, existence
-ant	one who	assistant, servant
-el, -et, -ette	little	satchel, locket, cigarette
-er, -eer, -ier	one who	baker, engineer, furrier
-ess	the female	goddess, princess, waitress
-fy	to make	glorify, purify, simplify
-icle, -sel	little	particle, morsel
-less	without	careless, guiltless, merciless
-ling	little	codling, gosling, darling
-ment	state of being	merriment, enjoyment
-ock	little	hillock, bittock
-oon, -on	large	saloon, balloon, flagon
-ory	a place for	dormitory, factory
-ous	full of	famous, glorious, momentous

Exercises on Derivations

1. Underline **the root parts** of the following words and give their meanings:

   century, December, factory, manual, navigate, suspend, pedal, export, describe, tentacles.

2. Underline **the prefixes** in the following words and give their meanings:

   anteroom, bicycle, circumference, contradict, forenoon, international, postscript, submarine, transport, unknown.

3. Underline **the suffixes** in the following words and give their meanings:

   heiress, cigarette, explorer, simplify, duckling, careless, edible, attendant, decorator, courageous.

General Knowledge

In the following list many questions can be answered by one word. Wherever possible, do so.

1. A boy who frightens weaker boys. *bully*
2. A number of soldiers. *Army*
3. The men and women who work on a ship. *crew*
4. Children in a school. ~~scho~~ *students*
5. A man who protects sheep. *shepard*
6. The low ground between two hills.
7. A place where pupils are educated. *school*
8. A ship which travels below the surface of the sea. *submarine*
9. A place for storing a car. *garage*
10. A small leaf. *leaflet*
11. A mammal that can fly. *bat*
12. A field in which fruit trees grow. *farm*
13. An instrument for measuring time. *clock*
14. From what do we make butter? *oil*
15. A man who makes things out of wood. *carpenter*
16. A fertile place in the desert. *oasis*
17. A man who pretends to be good. *hippocrite*
18. A person who is always boasting. *braggart*
19. A stream which flows into a river. *tributary*
20. A hundred years. *century*
21. Name an instrument for telling direction. *compass*
22. What are the steps of a ladder called? *rungs*
23. Name two spotted animals. *cheetah leopard*
24. A doctor who performs operations. *surgeon*
25. What is the front part of a ship called? *bow*
26. Headgear worn by some inhabitants of India. *turban*
27. A place where beer is made. *brenary*
28. What is daybreak sometimes termed? *dawn*
29. A man who draws and paints. *artist*
30. Fish with the bones taken out. *fught*
31. A shallow crossing in a river. *ford*
32. Two creatures which see well in the dark. *bats, owls*
33. What is the meaning of plume? *feather*
34. Name any American money. *cent*
35. Girl or woman who serves at table. *waitress*
36. A person who by desire lives alone. *hermit*
37. What do we call the breaking of a bone? *fracture*

38. Name two shellfish. *prawn, crab*
39. What is the flesh of a sheep called? *mutton*
40. The first meal of the day. *breakfast*
41. The city which has the Eiffel Tower. *Paris*
42. Name of metal container for oil. *drum*
43. Place in which photographs are taken.
44. A place where people are buried. *cemetary*
45. Another name for a policeman. *cop*
46. Name three "string" instruments. *guitar, ukele, piano*
47. Name the imaginary line round the middle of the earth. *eqator*
48. An instrument which measures heat and cold. *thermometer*
49. From what do we make cheese? *milk*
50. Name the five human senses. *sight, hearing, smell, taste, touch*
51. What kind of fish is a kipper? *herring*
52. Type of footwear in hot countries. *sandals, slip-flops*
53. A place where whisky is made. *distillery*
54. The most accurate kind of clock in the world. *atomic clock*
55. Name three infectious diseases. *polio, measels, whooping cough*
56. What lights must a steamer show at night? *red, green, white*
57. Name two striped animals. *zebra, tiger*
58. Goods carried out of a country. *export*
59. A place where birds are kept. *aviary*
60. Person who gives life in a good cause.
61. The air surrounding the earth. *atmosphere*
62. A person who saves and hoards money. *miser*
63. A religious song. *prayer? hymn?*
64. How does a fish breathe in water? *gills*
65. Name the colours of the rainbow. *red, orange, yellow, green, blue*
66. What is the small top room of a house? *attic*
67. Which is Britain's fiercest wild bird? *eagle*
68. What is the national dress of Scotland? *kilt*
69. A three-sided figure. *triangle*
70. A place where aeroplanes are kept. *airport*
71. Meaning of "The Seven Seas". *oceans of the world*
72. A vessel for holding flowers. *vase*
73. What is the meaning of steed? *horse*
74. Name the patron saint of England. *St George*
75. A person who cannot hear or speak. *deaf or mute*
76. A room on board a ship. *cabin*
77. A soldier with three stripes on each arm. *sergeant*

78. A person who takes the place of another. *substitute*
79. How many legs has a fly? *six*
80. Name four kinds of tree. *oak, apple, pine, beech*
81. A place where iron goods are made. *foundry*
82. Name four great deserts. *Gobi, Sahara*
83. Name three animals living mostly in water. *dolphin whale shark*
84. A man who does tricks with cards. *conjuror*
85. Water which has turned into gas. *steam*
86. The young that hatch from insect eggs. *larvae*
87. What is the flesh of a pig called? *pork*
88. Scottish loch in which there is said to be a monster. *Loch Ness*
89. Goods taken into a country. *import*
90. A place where leather is made. *tannery*
91. Another name for a donkey. *ass*
92. Machine which makes electricity. *dynamo*
93. What is milk-fat called? *cream*
94. What is wind? *moving air*
95. What is ackee? *a fruit that's cooked*
96. What is a tripod? *a three-legged stand for a camera*
97. Name an alcoholic drink made from sugar cane. *rum*
98. What is the flesh of the deer called? *venison*
99. Name for smuggled goods. *contraband*
100. What language was spoken by the ancient Romans? *latin*
101. A place where chickens are hatched. *incubator*
102. What is an astronaut? *a person that goes into space*
103. What are the primary colours? *red, yellow, blue*
104. Of what wood is a cricket bat made? *willow*
105. Name quick ways of sending messages. *phone, text, email*
106. What is the Milky Way? *a band of stars stretching across the sky.*
107. What was Guyana formerly called? *British Guyana*
108. Place where gas is stored. *gas holder*
109. Who were the Caribs? *Caribbean*
110. Explain lbw. *leg before wicket*
111. What is a boneshaker? *bicycle that jolts person*
112. Which is the lightest common metal? *aluminium*
113. What does NASA do? *send rockets into space*
114. Where is the longest wall in the world? *Great wall of china*
115. What is the capital of Cuba? *Havana*
116. A place where fish are kept. *Aquarium*
117. Who was Man Friday? *Robin Crusoe servant*

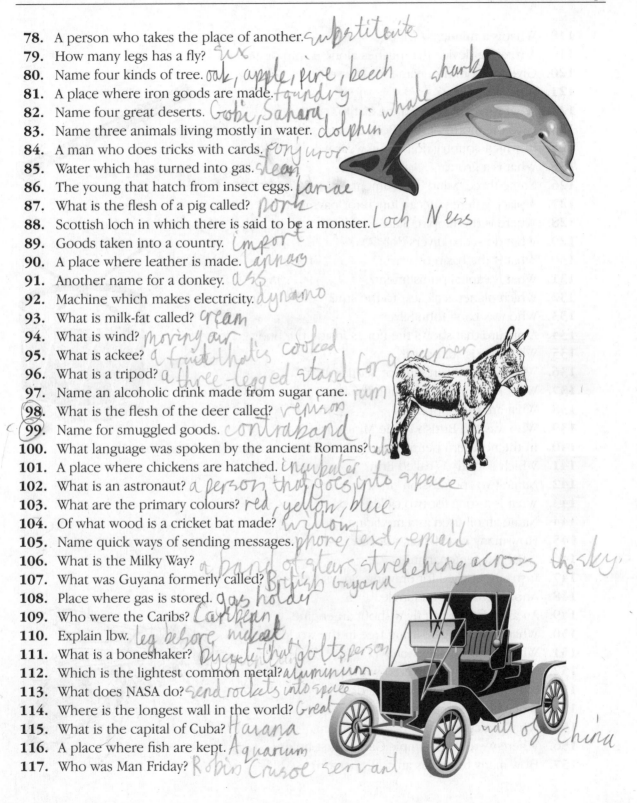

118. What is a mimic? *imitates someones actions*
119. A rotating device that pushes along a ship or aircraft. *propeller*
120. Give the common name for the spine. *backbone*
121. What is a planet? *a heavenly body that revolves around the sun*
122. What is meant by scuttling a ship? *deliberately sinking*
123. Give the motto of the (Boy) Scout Association. *Be prepared*
124. In which country do people wear wooden shoes? *Holland*
125. What is a grotto? *a picturesee cave*
126. Name three "wind" instruments. *flute, recorder, clarinet*
127. A place where you can lunch for payment. *restaurant*
128. Where is the Empire State Building? *New York*
129. What do scuba divers do? *explore under the sea*
130. What is the basin of a river? *all the land drained by a river*
131. What is capital punishment? *death by a crime*
132. Which planet is closest to the sun? *Mercury*
133. Who was Long John Silver? *a character pirate in treasure island*
134. A picture that shows the bones inside the body. *X-ray*
135. What side is starboard? *right*
136. Who is the patron saint of Scotland? *st Andrew*
137. What is meant by "crossing the line"? *sailing across the equator*
138. What are the Antipodes? *a group of Australia and New Zealand*
139. Who was the British Prime Minister in 2003? *Tony Blair*
140. In the northern hemisphere, which month contains the longest day? *June*
141. Which country is called Erin? *Ireland*
142. Name two "percussion" instruments. *drum tambourine*
143. What is a song for two called? *duet*
144. Name an oil used as a medicine. *castor oil*
145. How many in a "Baker's dozen"? *thirteen*
146. What is a centenarian? *aged 100 years or more*
147. Instrument used for drawing circles. *compass*
148. Another name for a jungle. *forest*
149. An aircraft that can fly without an engine. *glider*
150. What is the longest-living tree in the world? *redwood (s*
151. Which insect makes honey? *bee*
152. Name any animal covered with spines. *hedgehog*
153. When is the signal "SOS" used? *emergency*
154. When is Christmas Day? *25th December*
155. What is a cutlass? *a short sword*
156. Where were the Olympic Games first held? *Athens*
157. How many teeth has an adult person? *32*

158. Who is the patron saint of Ireland? *Patrick*
159. What do we call water when solid? *Ice*
160. What is a loom? *weaving machine*
161. Name any "pouched" animals. *kangaroo*
162. What is a fjord? *a deep inlet of water*
163. An instrument for seeing tiny objects. *microscope*
164. Who was David Livingstone? *an explorer of Africa*
165. In the northern hemisphere, which month contains the shortest day? *December*
166. Lemons, oranges and grapefruit are all *citric* fruits.
167. Name five common garden flowers. *rose, tulip, pansy, daisy, lily*
168. Group of countries including Sweden, Norway and Denmark.
169. What is a storey? *A floor*
170. Which animal is called the "King of Beasts"? *lion*
171. Who is the patron saint of Wales? *St David*
172. A funny drawing of general interest. *cartoon*
173. Where did the Incas live? *in Peru*
174. Another name for an airman. *aviator*
175. What is a burnous? *hooded cloak worn by Arab*
176. What is a bed on board a ship called? *bunk*
177. How many sides does a hexagon have? *six*
178. In which country are the Great Lakes found? *Canada*
179. What is a quadruped? *four footed animals*
180. Which animal covers great distances without water? *camel*
181. What is a hobo? *American for homeless*
182. Group of animals to which apes, monkeys and man belong. *primates*
183. What is a rickshaw? *carriage drawn by a man*
184. What kind of vegetable are cassavas, yams and sweet potatoes? *tubers*
185. A number of icebergs. *ice pack*
186. City famous for high buildings. *New York*
187. Another name for an aeroplane. *Jet*
188. What is a weather satellite? *a piece of equipment that sends information*
189. Name the insect which carries malaria fever. *mosquito*
190. What is the yellow part of an egg called? *yolk*
191. Who was Mars? *a roman god of war*
192. When is a person said to be myopic? *short sighted*
193. Name given to a sailor's map. *chart*
194. What is the skin of the orange called? *peal*
195. Crabs, lobster and prawns are all *crustations*
196. Another word meaning remedy. *cure*
197. Soldiers on horseback. *cavalry*

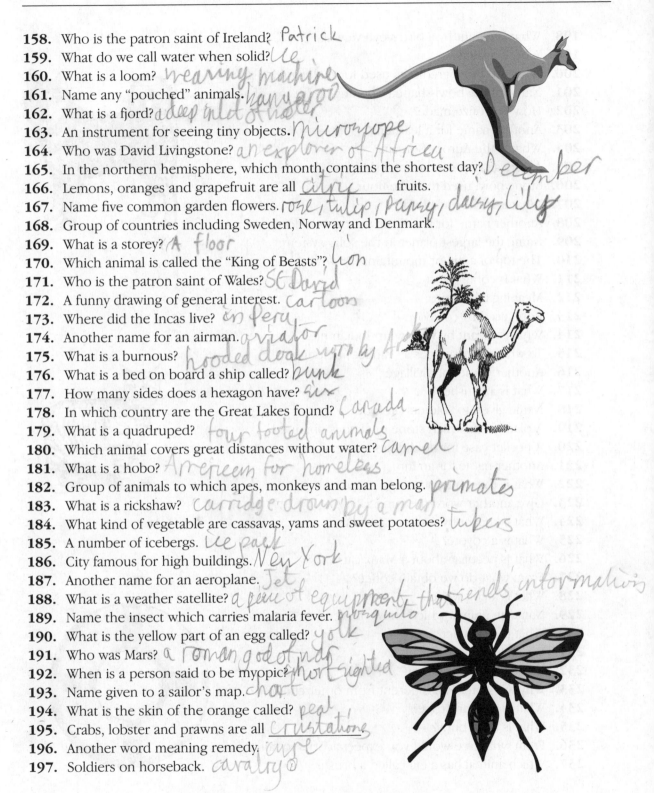

198. What is meant by a bird's-eye view? *a view from above*

199. Who is a sheik? *a Arab chief*

200. What are the ingredients used for making tea? *teabag, sugar, boiling water, milk*

201. Name of the bowl-shaped opening at the top of a volcano. *crater*

202. How is bronze made? *copper and tin*

203. Another name for a learner. *student*

204. What is the Aurora Borealis? *Northern Lights*

205. American dog used to pull sledges. *husky*

206. Stone bowl used to make flour. *Mortar*

207. What is a Thermos flask? *for keeping things warm or cold*

208. Another name for a way out sign above door. *exit*

209. Name the largest planet in the solar system. *Jupiter*

210. The top of a hill or mountain. *summit*

211. What is coral? *an animal in the sea*

212. Meaning of umpire. *a referee*

213. Rope used by cowboy. *lariat*

214. What is meant by walking in Indian file? *one behind the other*

215. To what country does a "Yankee" belong? *America*

216. Another name for a village. *hamlet*

217. What is a banshee? *a spirit who forewarned death*

218. Name given to soldiers on foot. *infantry*

219. A place from which stone or slate is obtained. *quarry*

220. A pocket case for holding money and documents. *wallet*

221. Another name for an inn. *hotel*

222. What is the white of an egg called? *albumen*

223. Give another word meaning salary. *sum of wages*

224. What is meant by walking abreast? *side by side*

225. What is a coyote? *American dog*

226. What is peculiar about a Manx cat? *it doesn't have a tail*

227. From what do we obtain coffee? *coffee bean*

228. What is a cog wheel? *a gear that has teeth*

229. Name an animal which chews the cud. *cow*

230. What is a cataract? *eye disease*

231. Which letters are vowels? *a, e, i, o, u,*

232. Name any beast of prey. *lion*

233. Why was Peter Pan different from other children? *he does not grow old*

234. What is a lunar probe? *equipment used for moon...*

235. What is a life buoy? *floating device to save people*

236. From what tree would you expect acorns to fall? *oak*

237. Which animal has a tail called a brush? *a fox*

238. What is a gondola? *a boat*
239. From what do we obtain cider? *apples*
240. What is a carnivorous creature? *animal that eats flesh*
241. Remedy for stings. *ointment*
242. Name the ABC islands. *Aruba, Bonare, Curac*
243. What is the handrail for a stair called? *banistar*
244. What is a nuclear power station? *atomic reactor generating electricity*
245. A clergyman's house is called a _*vicarage*_.
246. What is savannah? *African grassland*
247. What is the capital of England? *London*
248. Where is the "New World"? *America*
249. Name an animal with a very long neck. *giraffe*
250. What is veal? *baby cow*
251. Medical supplies used to treat cuts. *ointment*
252. Which is the biggest ocean in the world? *pacific*
253. Name an insect which appears to carry a lamp. *glow worm*
254. What is a nightmare? *a bad dream*
255. Which creatures have antlers? *reindeer, moose, stag*
256. What is a hod? *brick holder*
257. What were the kings of the Ancient Egyptians called? *pharohs*
258. Name given to a young tree. *sapling*
259. What is the middle part of an apple called? *core*

Fastenings

Name things fastened by the following:

belt	glue	mortar	solder
bolt	handcuffs	nail	staple
braces	harness	padlock	strap and buckle
brooch	hawsers	paste	string
button	hinge	peg	strut
cable	hook and eye	pin	tack
cement	lace	putty	thread
chain	latch	rivet	twine
clip	lock	rope	zip
cord			

Useful Information

Human Beings differ in a number of inherited features, e.g. skin colour; shape of nose, eyes, lips; type and colour of hair. They are:

Yellow featured. Yellow, copper skin; fairly broad nose, low bridge; slanting eyes; black hair. Chinese, Japanese, Siberian and South-East Asians, Inuits, Native Americans, Laplanders. Most numerous.

White featured. Pink, olive, light brown skin; high narrow nose; eyes light, more recessed; hair wavy or straight, more beard. Europeans and their American descendants, South-West Asians, Indians, other South Asians and some Pacific islanders.

Black featured. Black or dark brown skin; broad nose, thick lips; black, brown curly hair, less beard. African peoples and American descendants, Afro-Caribbeans, etc., Papuans and some other Pacific islanders.

The **Principal Languages of the World** are as follows (arranged according to the number speaking each): Chinese, English, Russian, Western Hindi, Spanish, German, French, Japanese, Portuguese and Italian.

The **Continents** are: Europe, Asia, Africa, America and Australia.

The **Oceans** are: Atlantic, Pacific, Indian, Arctic and Antarctic.

The **Largest Islands** (other than the continents) are: Greenland, New Guinea, Borneo, Madagascar and Baffin Island.

The **Greatest Lakes** are: Caspian Sea (Asia: borders Russia and Iran among others), Lake Superior (North America), Victoria Nyanza (Central Africa), Aral Sea (Asia: between Kazakstan and Uzbekistan), Lake Huron (North America) and Lake Michigan (North America).

The **Highest Mountains of the World** are all in the Himalayan Mountain Range in Northern India. They are: Mt Everest, Mt Godwin-Austin (K-2), Mt Kangchenjunga, Mt Nanga Parbat and Mt Kamet.

The **Longest Rivers** are: Missouri-Mississippi (United States), Amazon (Brazil), Nile (Egypt), Yangtse (China), Lena (Russia), Zaire (Central Africa), Niger (West Africa) and Yenesei (Russia).

The **Largest Cities of the World** are: Tokyo (Japan), Mexico City (Mexico), New York (USA), Sao Paulo (Brazil), Mumbai (India), Shanghai (China), Calcutta (India), Buenos Aires (Argentina), Beijing (China), Seoul (South Korea), Cairo (Egypt) and Los Angeles (USA).

Various Countries – The Peoples – Their Languages

Country	People	Language
Australia	Australians	English, Aboriginal languages
Bangladesh	Bangladeshis	Bengali
Belgium	Belgians	Flemish, French
Bulgaria	Bulgarians	Bulgarian
Canada	Canadians	English, French
China (People's Rep.)	Chinese	Chinese
Czech Republic	Czechs, Slovaks	Czech
Denmark	Danes	Danish
Egypt	Egyptians	Arabic
England	English	English
Finland	Finns	Finnish
France	French	French
Germany	Germans	German
Greece	Greeks	Greek
Holland	Dutch	Dutch
Hungary	Hungarians	Hungarian
India	Indians	Hindi, English
Iran	Iranians	Farsi
Ireland (Eire)	Irish	English, Gaelic
Israel	Jews, Arabs	Hebrew, Arabic
Italy	Italians	Italian
Jamaica	Jamaicans	English
Japan	Japanese	Japanese
Kenya	Kenyan	Swahili, English
Malawi	Malawians	CiCewa
Mexico	Mexicans	Spanish
New Zealand	New Zealanders	English, Maori
Nigeria	Nigerians	Yoruba, Hausa, Ibo
Pakistan	Pakistanis	Urdu
Poland	Poles	Polish
Portugal	Portuguese	Portuguese
Russia	Russians	Russian

Country	People	Language
Saudi Arabia	Arabs	Arabic
Scotland	Scots	English, Gaelic
Singapore	Singaporeans	Malay, Chinese, Tamil, English
Slovakia	Slovaks	Slovak, Hungarian
South Africa	South Africans	English, Afrikaans, Zulu, Xhosa
Spain	Spanish	Spanish, Basque, Catalan
Sri Lanka	Srilankans	Singhalese, Tamil, English
Switzerland	Swiss	French, German, Italian
Turkey	Turks	Turkish
United States	Americans	English, Spanish
Wales	Welsh	English, Cymric
Zimbabwe	Zimbabweans	Shona, Ndebele, English

Origin of Certain Place Names

Africa was so named by the Romans after the Afri tribe of Tunisia.

America is named after Amerigo Vespucci, who explored parts of the coastline of the New World, shortly after its discovery by Columbus.

Asia, the largest continent, takes its name from the district behind Smyrna in Turkey. We sometimes refer to the eastern part of the continent as the "Orient" (Land of the Rising Sun).

Australia means the "Southern Continent". National Emblems – Kangaroo, Emu, Mimosa.

Europe – some say it was named Eref by the Phoenicians, meaning "The Land of the Setting Sun" and sometimes referred to as the "Occident". Others say it was named after Europus, a town in Macedonia.

Canada – from Native American word "Kannata", meaning "a number of settlers' huts". National Emblems – Maple Leaf, Beaver.

China (The Chinese people seldom use this name but generally refer to the Province concerned.) The word is said to have come from "Tsin", the ruler who built the Great Wall of China. National Emblems – Dragon, Plum Blossom.

England – land of the Angles, who invaded and conquered South Britain in the 5th century. National Emblems – Lion, Rose, Bulldog.

France (Old name Gaul – land of the Gauls.) Present name from the Franks, who later conquered the country. National Emblems – Lily, Cock, Eagle.

Germany – "Germanus" (neighbour), a Roman word borrowed from the Gauls. Germans call their country "Deutschland". National Emblems – Eagle, Corn Flower.

India – the land through which the River Indus has its course. National Emblems – Elephant, Star, Lotus, Jasmine.

Ireland (Gaelic name – Eire) – land of the Irish tribe. National Emblems – Shamrock, Harp.

Italy (= vitalia) – means "cattle or pasture land". National Emblems – Eagle, Lily, Laurel wreath.

Japan – The Japanese always use the word "Nippon" and both mean "The Land of the Rising Sun". National Emblems – Chrysanthemum, Rising Sun.

New Zealand (New Sea Land) – so named by a Dutch explorer after Zealand – a part of Holland. National Emblems – Kiwi, Fern.

Nigeria – Nigeria was named after the River Niger.

Russia – land of the tribe of Russ. National Emblems – Hammer and Sickle, Five-pointed Star.

Scotland (Old name Caledonia). Present name from the Scots, a north of Ireland tribe, who invaded and gradually became masters of the whole country. National Emblems – Lion, Thistle.

South Africa (see "Africa"). National Emblems – Springbok, Real Yellowwood.

Spain – English form of the word "Hispania" or "España". The name comes from "Shapan" (rabbit land), as the Phoenicians found the country overrun with these animals. National Emblems – Red Carnation, Pomegranate.

USA (see "America"). National Emblems – Eagle, Buffalo, Golden Rod.

Turkey – land of the Turks. National Emblem – Star and Crescent.

Wales (Old name Cymru – land of the Cymry tribe). Present name is derived from Anglo-Saxon word meaning "land of the foreigner". National Emblems – Leek, Daffodil, Dragon.

Various Countries and their Capitals

Country	Capital	Country	Capital
Albania	Tirana	Kenya	Nairobi
Argentina	Buenos Aires	Netherlands	Amsterdam
Australia	Canberra	New Zealand	Wellington
Belgium	Brussels	Nigeria	Abuja
Belize	Belmopan	Norway	Oslo
Brazil	Brasilia	Pakistan	Islamabad
Bulgaria	Sofia	Poland	Warsaw
Canada	Ottawa	Portugal	Lisbon
China	Beijing	Rumania	Bucharest
Colombia	Bogotá	Russia	Moscow
Cuba	Havana	Scotland	Edinburgh
Czech Republic	Prague	South Africa	Cape Town
Denmark	Copenhagen	Spain	Madrid
Egypt	Cairo	Sri Lanka	Colombo
England	London	Sweden	Stockholm
France	Paris	Switzerland	Berne
Germany	Berlin	Thailand	Bangkok
Greece	Athens	Trinidad	Port of Spain
Hungary	Budapest	Turkey	Ankara
India	New Delhi	Uganda	Kampala
Ireland	Dublin	United States	Washington DC
Italy	Rome	Uruguay	Montevideo
Jamaica	Kingston	Venezuala	Caracas
Japan	Tokyo	Zimbabwe	Harare

Currencies of Various Countries

Country	Currency	Country	Currency
Argentina	peso, centavo	Luxembourg	euro, cent
Australia	dollar, cent	Mexico	peso, centavo
Belgium	euro, cent	Netherlands	euro, cent
Canada	dollar, cent	New Zealand	dollar, cent
China	yuan, fen	Nigeria	naira, kobo
Denmark	krone, øre	Poland	zloty, grosz
Egypt	pound, piastre	Portugal	euro, cent
France	euro, cent	Russia	rouble, kopeck
Germany	euro, cent	South Africa	rand, cent
Greece	euro, cent	Spain	euro, cent
India	rupee, paisa	Switzerland	franc, centime
Italy	euro, cent	Turkey	lira, juru
Japan	yen, sen	United States	dollar, cent
Kenya	shilling, cent	Vietnam	dong

Exercises on Useful Information

Do you know:

1. With which **country** or **people** each of the following is associated?

Ali	Foreign Legion	moccasins	scimitar
Balmoral	furs	mummies	shamrock
Beefeater	gaucho	onions	sombrero
beret	Hans	oranges	spaghetti
bolas	heather	ostrich	tea
boomerang	ice cream	Pablo	tigers
butter	John Bull	reggae	tomahawk
cheese	kangaroo	reindeer	tulips
chop-sticks	kilt	rickshaw	turban
chrysanthemum	lariat	Rising Sun	Uncle Sam
clogs	leek	rose	vodka
corn flower	lotus flower	salmon	watches
cowboy	macaroni	sandals	whisky
daffodil	Marianne	sari	windmills
fez	Midnight Sun		

2. With which **countries** do you associate the following beasts of burden?

Egypt, Spain, India, Peru, India, Tibet, Greenland, Arabia, USA, Nepal, Finland

camel, dog, donkey, dromedary, elephant, horse, llama, mule, ox, reindeer, yak.

3. Who use (or used) the following kinds of boats?

Welsh, Nomads, Chinese, Chinese, Native America, Arabs, Venetians, Inuit

canoe, coracle, dhow, galleon, gondola, junk, kayak, sampan.

4. What **national** names are often attached to the following?

Example: Kenyan coffee. **Scotch** broth.

Turkish, Persian, Dutch, Indian, Spanish, Chinese, Jamaica, German, Irish, Indian

baths, carpets, cheese, curry, onions, noodles, rum, sausage, stew, tea.

5. Who use (or used) these weapons?

Aborigine, Whalers, Pirates, Policemen, Native Americans

boomerang, cutlass, harpoon, tomahawk, truncheon.

6. In what **country** would you be if your journey was called a

Kenya, Saudi Arabia, Canada, South Africa

a) safari, b) mush, c) hajj, d) trek?

7. In which **countries** might men have each of the following names?

Angus MacDonald, Tom Smith, Evan Jones, Patrick O'Neil, Chang Wu,
Fritz Schmidt, Ivan Petrovitch, Juan Caballero, Pierre Sablon, Hans Brinker.

Exercises on Useful Information continued

8. **In which town and country is each of the following situated?**

   Cleopatra's Needle, Colosseum, Eiffel Tower, Leaning Tower, Nelson's Column, Pyramids, The Golden Gate, The Golden Horn, The Houses of Parliament, The Kremlin, The Statue of Liberty, The Sphinx, The Taj Mahal, The Bridge of Sighs, The White House, The Vatican.

9. **In which countries are the following mountains situated?**

   Blue Mountains, Cotopaxi, Mt Everest, Fujiyama, Mt Blanc, Kilimanjaro, Table Mountain, The Rockies, Uhuru Peak, Vesuvius.

10. **With which countries are the following famous people associated?**

    Nelson Mandela, Captain Cook, Bob Marley, George Washington, Jomo Kenyatta, Mao Zedong, Ned Kelly, Indira Gandhi, Duke Ellington, Diego Maradona, Pele, Florence Nightingale, Mother Teresa, Stalin, Hitler, Aretha Franklin, Joan of Arc, Julius Caesar, Martin Luther King, Napoleon, Kemal Ataturk, Mozart, Fidel Castro, Yasser Arafat, Peter the Great, General De Gaulle.

11. **To what countries do the following names (seen on foreign stamps) apply?**

    Argentina, Belgique, Danmark, Eire, Suomi, France, Deutschland, Nederland, Italia, Norge, Polska, Romania, España, Sverige, Suisse or Helvetia.

The Wonders of the World

In olden times travellers who visited foreign lands generally brought back amazing tales of the wonderful sights they had seen on their journeys. The most famous of these sights became known as the Seven Wonders.

1. The Pyramids of Egypt.
2. The Hanging Gardens of Babylon.
3. The Tomb of Mausolus at Halicarnassus.
4. The Temple of Artemis (Diana) at Ephesus.
5. The Colossus at Rhodes.
6. The Statue of Zeus (Jupiter) at Olympia.
7. The Pharos Lighthouse at Alexandria.

Of the above **Seven Wonders of the Ancient World** only the Great Pyramids of Egypt survive today.

In the Middle Ages people considered that there existed other sights quite as wonderful and named the following:

1. The Colosseum of Rome.
2. The Leaning Tower of Pisa.
3. The Catacombs of Alexandria.
4. The Great Wall of China.
5. Stonehenge.
6. The Porcelain Tower of Nanking.
7. The Mosque of St Sophia in Constantinople (Istanbul).

All of these **Wonders of the Middle Ages** (some of which are much older than the Middle Ages) still stand or have remains which can still be seen.

Today it would be impossible to make a completely satisfactory list of Seven Wonders as we have all seen or heard of many amazing man-made structures and scientific marvels. Under these two headings the following are remarkable enough to be included in any list of **Wonders of the Modern World**:

Man-made Structures
1. Simplon Tunnel.
2. The Skyscrapers of New York (USA).
3. The Boulder Dam of Colorado (USA).
4. The Panama Canal (Central America).
5. The Golden Gate Bridge at San Francisco (USA).
6. The Taj Mahal at Agra (India).
7. North Sea Oil drilling rigs and production platforms.

Scientific Marvels

1. Internal combustion engine.
2. Concorde.
3. Space travel.
4. Anaesthetics.
5. Heart surgery.
6. Bio-engineering.
7. Radio.
8. Radar.
9. Fibre-optics communication.
10. Television.
11. Lasers.
12. Computers.

Science Vocabulary

1. doctor's "listening" instrument	stethoscope
2. magnifies tiny objects	microscope
3. makes distant objects look bigger, nearer	telescope
4. measures heat and cold	thermometer
5. measures heat of the body	clinical thermometer
6. indicates the weather	barometer
7. measures gas or electricity used	meter
8. helps the voice to carry	megaphone
9. picks up sound for sending out again	microphone
10. carries messages by wire	telephone
11. carries sound without use of wires	radio
12. carries messages by wire across the sea	cable
13. takes photographs	camera
14. takes photographs through the body	X-rays
15. glasses used for bettering the eyesight	spectacles
16. instrument used for telling time	watch
17. tells if a thing is horizontal	spirit-level
18. tells if a thing is vertical	plumb-line
19. gives direction	compass
20. a sailor's map	chart
21. a ship which can travel below the water	submarine
22. attracts iron	magnet
23. makes electricity	dynamo / alternator
24. ship's engine which works by steam	turbine
25. a machine for measuring time	clock
26. measures angles in surveying	theodolite
27. instrument for drawing circles	compasses
28. releases over-pressure of steam	safety-valve
29. machine used in business for letter-writing	computer / word processor
30. causes the spark in motor engine	magneto / distributor

Sound travels 1.6 km in 5 seconds.
Light travels approximately 300,000 km in 1 second.
Light takes 8 minutes to reach the Earth from the Sun.
36 km per hour is equal to 10 m per second.
1 litre of water weighs 1 kg.
1 nautical mile is 1.85 km.

Spelling Lists

Home
attic
bolster
cellar
chimney
curtains
cushion
detergent
hearth
kitchen
lobby
mattress
meter
mirror
parlour
pillow
poker
saucer
scullery
towel
tumbler

People
adult
ancestors
aunt
babies
children
comrade
cousin
friend
guest
hostess
maiden
nephew
niece
orphan
parents
relation
uncle
visitor
widower
youth

Body
ankles
arteries
exercise
forehead
heart
knees
knuckles
limbs
lungs
muscles
nostrils
shoulder
skeleton
skull
stomach
thigh
throat
tongue
veins
wrist

Food
bacon
biscuits
bread
butter
cheese
chocolate
cocoa
coffee
margarine
marmalade
mutton
porridge
pudding
sago
salmon
sandwich
sausages
steak
sugar
venison

Clothing
braid
cloak
costume
cotton
flannel
gabardine
garments
jacket
linen
lingerie
muslin
petticoat
satin
stocking
trousers
tweed
velour
velvet
waistcoat
woollen

Trades
butcher
carpenter
chemist
clothier
doctor
draper
druggist
engineer
grocer
journalist
lawyer
mason
mechanic
plumber
purveyor
riveter
sawyer
sculptor
tailor
wright

Travel (1)
aeroplane
airship
balloon
bicycle
brakes
carriage
coach
cruise
electricity
engine
express
fares
gangway
guard
helicopter
label
locomotive
luggage
machine
parcel

Travel (2)
passengers
pedals
pier
platform
purser
saloon
seaplane
signal
skis
sledge
sleigh
steerage
steward
tourist
tramway
traveller
tunnel
vehicle
wagons
whistles

Land	Sea	Sky	Coast
cape	billows	altitude	bathing
cliff	breakers	astronomy	beach
continent	breakwater	atmosphere	billows
country	channel	cloudy	breeze
headland	crest	comet	cliffs
hillock	fjord	creation	cockles
island	harbour	crescent	costume
marsh	inlet	dawn	diving
mound	lagoon	eclipse	herring
mountain	lake	hazy	lobster
pampas	loch	heavens	mussels
peninsula	ocean	horizon	pier
plain	river	midnight	rowing
prairie	rivulet	planet	seaweed
precipice	sea	solar	shingle
summit	streamlet	sunset	swimmer
tundra	torrent	telescope	view
valley	tributary	twilight	whelks
veldt	trough	universe	winkles
volcano	waves	zenith	wreck

Time	Sport	School	Hospital
ancient	badminton	calendar	accident
annual	bowls	ceiling	casualty
August	boxing	chalk	chloroform
autumn	cricket	composition	disease
century	fencing	copies	doctor
Christmas	football	cupboard	fever
dawn	golf	dictation	infection
Easter	hockey	easel	massage
era	polo	grammar	medicine
February	putting	history	ointment
gloaming	rounders	hymns	operation
January	rugby	interval	paralysis
minutes	shinty	partition	physician
modern	skating	pastels	plaster
punctual	sleighing	pencil	poison
Saturday	sprinting	picture	sterilise
September	swimming	poetry	surgeon
Thursday	tennis	pupil	thermometer
Tuesday	wrestling	scholar	tonic
Wednesday	yachting	teacher	ward

Mammals (1)	Mammals (2)	Mammals (3)	Dogs
ape	goat	otter	Airedale
armadillo	gorilla	ox	Alsatian
badger	hare	panther	bloodhound
bat	hedgehog	pig	borzoi
bear	hippopotamus	porcupine	bulldog
beaver	horse	puma	collie
buffalo	hyena	rabbit	dachshund
bull	jackass	rat	Dalmatian
camel	jaguar	reindeer	greyhound
cat	kangaroo	seal	Newfoundland
cow	leopard	sheep	Pekinese
deer	lion	skunk	pointer
dog	llama	squirrel	Pomeranian
donkey	lynx	stoat	poodle
dromedary	mole	tiger	retriever
elephant	mongoose	walrus	Saint Bernard
ferret	monkey	weasel	setter
fox	moose	whale	sheepdog
gazelle	mouse	yak	spaniel
giraffe	mule	zebra	terrier

Birds (1)	Birds (2)	Birds (3)	Fish
albatross	hawk	redshank	cod
blackbird	heron	robin	dogfish
budgerigar	jackdaw	rook	eel
canary	kingfisher	sandpiper	flounder
chaffinch	lapwing	seagull	flying-fish
cormorant	magpie	skylark	goldfish
corncrake	moorhen	snipe	haddock
crane	nightingale	sparrow	halibut
crow	owl	starling	herring
cuckoo	oyster-catcher	stork	mackerel
curlew	parrot	swallow	pike
dipper	partridge	swan	plaice
duck	peewit	swift	roach
eagle	pelican	tern	salmon
falcon	penguin	thrush	shark
finch	pheasant	turkey	skate
flamingo	pigeon	vulture	sole
gannet	plover	wagtail	swordfish
goose	puffin	woodpecker	trout
guillemot	raven	wren	whiting

Trees	Flowers (1)	Flowers (2)	Insects
apple	aster	lotus	ant
ash	bluebell	lupin	bee
beech	buttercup	marigold	beetle
birch	carnation	narcissus	bug
cedar	chrysanthemum	orchid	butterfly
chestnut	crocus	pansy	centipede
elm	daffodil	peony	cricket
fir	dahlia	poppy	daddy-long-legs
hawthorn	daisy	primrose	dragonfly
larch	dandelion	queen-of-the-meadow	earwig
lime	forget-me-not	rhododendron	flea
maple	foxglove	rose	fly
oak	geranium	snowdrop	gnat
olive	gladiolus	sunflower	grasshopper
palm	honeysuckle	sweet pea	locust
pine	hyacinth	thistle	louse
poplar	iris	tulip	midge
rowan	lilac	violet	mosquito
sycamore	lily	wallflower	moth
yew	lily-of-the-valley	waterlily	wasp

Fruit	Vegetables	Minerals	Liquids
apple	bean	aluminium	acid
apricot	beetroot	brass	alcohol
banana	cabbage	bronze	beer
blackcurrant	carrot	coal	brine
bramble	cauliflower	copper	cider
cherry	celery	gold	cocoa
currant	cucumber	granite	coffee
damson	garlic	iron	lemonade
gooseberry	leek	lead	milk
grape	lettuce	marble	oil
lemon	onion	mercury	paraffin
melon	parsley	nickel	petrol
orange	parsnip	platinum	port
peach	pea	radium	sherry
pear	potato	silver	tea
pineapple	radish	slate	turpentine
plum	rhubarb	steel	vinegar
raspberry	sprout	sulphur	water
strawberry	tomato	tin	whisky
tomato	turnip	zinc	wine

General Tests

Test 1

1. Break down the following sentence into clauses:

When the girl returned from **London** she told **her** father **that** she had seen a **grizzly** bear which **performed** tricks in the circus.

(handwritten annotations: proper noun, pronoun, adjective, noun, verb)

2. Parse the words printed in **bold** type in Question 1.

3. a)   State the feminine of:

waiter, bachelor, horse, manservant, husband.

(handwritten: waitress, bacheless, wife, ladyservant)

   b)   Give the plural of:

knife, child, penny, sheep, piano.

(handwritten: knives, children, pennies, herd, pianos)

4. Insert the names of the creatures:

The _donkey_ brays.   The _owl_ hoots.
The _pig_ grunts.   The _monkey_ chatters.
The _frog_ croaks.   The _sheep_ bleats.
The _dog_ barks.   The _horse_ neighs.
The _wolf_ howls.   The _elephant_ trumpets.

5. Correct the following sentences:

   a)   He said that you done it. *(did)*
   b)   She is the biggest of the twins. *(elder)*
   c)   It was me that took the pencil.
   d)   The man went for to get the book.
   e)   A piano was sold to the lady with carved legs.

Test 2

1. Select from each of the following sentences the subordinate clause and tell its kind and relation:

   a)   The cottage where Burns was born stands **near** Ayr.
   b)   He told **me secretly** where he was going.
   c)   The **soldiers** slept where they found a **resting** place.

2. Parse the words printed in **bold** type in Question 1.

3. Supply the missing words:

> **Example:** As sharp as a needle.
>
> As black as _____   As fast as _____
>
> As meek as _____   As happy as _____
>
> As brave as _____   As keen as _____
>
> As sweet as _____   As steady as _____
>
> As cold as _____   As fit as _____

4. a)   Give the objective case of:

> I, he, you, we, they.

b)   Give the past tense of:

> does, hides, writes, sings, bites.

5. Change the clauses set in **bold** type into phrases:

a)   The child was in bed **before the sun had set**.

b)   Flowers will grow **where conditions are suitable**.

c)   Remember to write **when you arrive**.

d)   I saw her **when the clock struck four**.

e)   I am convinced **that he is sincere**.

Test 3

1. Break down the following sentence into clauses:

> **When** the gentleman arrived at his home he **discovered** that he had left **his** umbrella in the **train**.

2. Parse the words printed in **bold** type in Question 1.

3. Write down the Comparatives and Superlatives of:

> many, hot, evil, famous, little.

4. a)   Name the homes of the following:

> horse, hare, traveller, eagle, bee.

b)   By adding a prefix form words opposite in meaning to:

> possible, secure, welcome, use, legal.

5. Change all Singulars into Plurals and Verbs into Past Tense:

a)   The rabbit runs from the dog.

b)   The girl wears a blue dress.

c)   The sailor swims to his ship.

d)   He has a sharp knife.

e)   I keep my bird in a cage.

Test 4

1. Read the following sentence and then answer the questions below:

> When I heard that the man was seriously injured I resolved to help him in every way possible.

- a)   Write out the adverbial clause.
- b)   What parts of speech are: I, seriously, resolved, possible?
- c)   What part of the verb is **to help**?
- d)   What number is **him**?
- e)   What is the subject of **was injured**?
- f)   Write down the preposition in the sentence.

2. a)   Form nouns from:

> introduce, loyal, revive, ready, broad.

    b)   Form adjectives from:

> parent, reason, fortune, poet, winter.

3. Use any five of the following words (one for each sentence) to form short sentences:

> instinct, obstinate, traditional, respectively, occurrence, standard, respectable, resolved.

4. Put the correct prepositions in the blank spaces:
- a)   The boy was told not to meddle _____ the pencils.
- b)   She felt ashamed _____ herself.
- c)   The man took great pride _____ his garden.
- d)   The child has been lost _____ Thursday.
- e)   He hurried home _____ school.

5. What is meant by saying a person is:

a)	hard up,	f)	at rest,
b)	hard of hearing,	g)	lion-hearted,
c)	stuck up,	h)	ill-used,
d)	dead beat,	i)	an old salt,
e)	all ears,	(j)	out of sorts?

Test 5

1. Break down the following sentence into clauses:

> **We** were **thoroughly** alarmed when information reached us that the **train** in **which** our friends were travelling had been involved in a **serious** accident.

2. Parse the words printed in **bold** type in Question 1.

3. a) Some Christian names have popular short names, e.g.

> Robert – Bob, Catherine – Kate.

Give the short names for:

> Albert, Christina, Frederick, Patrick, Elizabeth.

  b) In which countries do the following peoples live?

> Dutch, Maoris, Inuit, Greeks, Welsh.

4. Punctuate and insert capital letters where necessary:

> do you think said my friend in a whisper that theres a chance of escape certainly i replied.

5. Insert the following phrases in their sentences:

> rack and ruin, thick and thin, head and shoulders, safe and sound, out and out.

  a) The ship reached harbour _____.
  b) The man was an _____ rascal.
  c) She is _____ taller than her brother.
  d) Later through foolishness he went to _____.
  e) The soldiers would follow their general through _____.

Test 6

1. Read the following sentence and then answer the questions below:

> When the man reached the garden gate he noticed that the old house in which he was born was in ruins.

  a) What parts of speech are:

> garden, that, which, was, ruins?

  b) Write out the principal clause.
  c) Write out the subordinate adjective clause.
  d) Name the kind of sentence.

2. In the following list of words, one word seems out of place. Underline the word you consider is wrong:

> Coat, hat, gloves, curtains, stockings.
> Blue, yellow, ruler, green, pink.
> Saw, envelope, plane, hammer, chisel.
> Anchor, rope, string, twine, cord.
> Needle, pin, scissors, thimble, spoon.

3. Where would you look to find:

> The address of a person?
> The position of a place?
> The meaning of a word?
> The day and date of the month?
> Something which happened the previous day?

4. Give the past tense and past participle of the following verbs:

> break, fly, hide, ring, swim.

5. What is meant in each of the following proverbs?
  a)   Let sleeping dogs lie.
  b)   Too many cooks spoil the broth.
  c)   Once bitten twice shy.

Test 7

1. Add a clause and name the kind of clause you add:
  a)   We ran for shelter _____.
  b)   When the rain stopped _____.
  c)   Mary told him _____.
  d)   The cunning fox _____ could not be caught.

2. Correct the following sentences:
  a)   Walk as quick as possible.
  b)   He has forgot the address.
  c)   Neither Tom or I can swim.
  d)   This end of the rope is the thickest.
  e)   The time was quarter past 9.

3. Make a noun from **strong**.
   Make a verb from **courage**.
   Make an adjective from **obey**.
   Give the opposite of **poverty**.
   Give a similar word to **mute**.

4. Medal, board, loose, waist, hoping, lose, meddle, hopping, bored, waste.

   Fill in the blank spaces of the following sentences, using the most suitable words from the above list:

   The teacher told the little boy not to _____ with the _____ as it had a _____ hinge. The child went over to the _____ paper bin _____ to find his pencil.

5. The following is written in the **singular number** and **present tense**. Change it into **plural number** and **past tense**.

   I have a cousin who stays on that little farm. He knows that I like to come here on my holiday.

Test 8

1. Read the following sentence carefully and then answer the questions below.

   When the soldiers reached the city walls they saw that the town which the enemy had completely ruined had been deserted for some time.

   a) Give the case and relation of: town, which, walls.
   b) What parts of speech are: city, that, reached, enemy, for, some?
   c) Write out the subordinate adverbial clause.

2. a) Give the opposites of:

      seldom, visible, praise, export, advance.

   b) Give similar words to:

      enemy, purchase, feeble, perceive, conceal.

3. Your answer in each case should be one word:
   a) A person who explores under the sea.
   b) Water which has turned into gas.
   c) Name of metal container for oil.
   d) A place where birds are kept.
   e) A vehicle that conveys the sick or injured to hospital.

4. Join the following ten words in pairs so that they form five sensible compound words:

   head, black, gentle, dust, egg, bin, ache, board, cup, man.

5. Complete these proverbs:
   a) A stitch in time _____
   b) A bird in the hand _____
   c) Birds of a feather _____
   d) A rolling stone _____
   e) First come _____

6. Give the meaning of:

   a.m., Co., BBC, PO, p.m., MP, UK, AD, USA, JP.

Test 9

1. Add a clause and name the kind of clause you add:
   a) The boys ran away _____.
   b) The lady _____ was my sister.
   c) The man saw _____ when he returned.
   d) _____ before the child arrived.

2. a) State the masculine of:

   witch, duck, aunt, vixen, wife.

   b) Give the singular of:

   loaves, armies, roofs, sheep, feet.

3. Use each of these verbs – frowned, mumbled, sang, chuckled, bowed, whispered, listened, smiled – once only to complete the following sentences:

a) He _____ tunefully.

b) He _____ angrily.

c) He _____ humbly.

d) He _____ indistinctly.

e) He _____ gleefully.

f) He _____ broadly.

g) He _____ attentively.

h) He _____ softly.

4. A number of sheep together is called a **flock**.

What name is given to a number of:

ships, insects, herring, angels, thieves, wolves, chickens, pups, players?

5. Make each pair of sentences into one sentence without using **and** or **but** or **so**.

a) The house was destroyed. It was built by Tom's father.

b) He works hard at his lesson. He wishes to succeed.

c) The men were walking quickly. The men saw me.

d) He heard the sound of music. He was passing the church.

e) The lady lost the book. She was going to the library.

Test 10

1. Read the sentences below and then answer the questions:

Our little hut was situated among the high mountains near the River Dee. Along the banks lay green pastures to which deer came frequently in winter.

a) What case is **hut**?

b) What kind of noun is **Dee**?

c) What part of speech is **our**?

d) Parse **among**.

e) What is the subject of **lay**?

f) Parse **frequently**.

g) What tense is **came**?

h) What part of speech is **which**?

i) What gender is **deer**?

j) What part of speech is **high**?

2. a) Form adjectives from: affection, nature, attraction, pride, value.

   b) State opposites of: success, arrive, often, sense, entrance.

3. Make sentences, one for each word, showing the correct use of:

coarse, course, root, route, rode, rowed, currant, current.

4. Rewrite the following correctly:

a boy said to his friend where are you going james oh replied the other i'm on my way home.

5. Give one word in place of each:
   a) A fertile place in the desert.
   b) A person who by desire lives alone.
   c) An instrument for measuring heat and cold.
   d) A person who looks on the bright side of things.
   e) A stream which flows into a river.

Test 11

1. a) Make a sentence containing **that he would come** as a noun clause.
   b) Make a sentence containing **which he bought** as an adjective clause.
   c) Make a sentence containing **when he reached the station** as an adverbial clause.

2. Give the:
   plural of **ox**
   feminine of **tiger**
   word for a young **swan**
   word for the traditional home of an **Inuit**
   adverb from **danger**.

3. Put in the suitable words in the spaces below:

Example: Little is to **Big** as **Dwarf** is to **Giant**.
Sheep is to **Mutton** as **Pig** is to _____.
High is to **Low** as _____ is to **Down**.
Soldier is to ._____ as **Sailor** is to **Navy**.
_____ is to **Herring** as **School** is to **Whales**.
Bee is to **Hive** as **Cow** is to _____.

4. Change the following **Complex Sentences** into **Simple Sentences**:

   a) There is a boy who is very proud.
   b) He spoke to me while he was passing.
   c) The girl who is intelligent gave the right answer.
   d) The man bought a boat which is very big.
   e) We received word that he was rescued.

5. With which countries do you associate the following famous people?

Robert the Bruce _____	George Washington _____
Stalin _____	Napoleon _____
Captain Cook _____	De Valera _____
David Livingstone _____	Jomo Kenyatta _____
Lloyd George _____	Gandhi _____

Test 12

1. Read the sentence and then answer the questions below:

When the boys who were playing in the park heard the school bell ringing loudly they were afraid that they would be late.

What parts of speech are:

who, park, loudly, school, that?

What part of the verb is **playing**?
What is the case of **bell**?
What is the number of **boys**?
What is the subject of **heard**?
What is the gender of **they**?

2. a) Give the gender of:

   lion, cousin, table, waitress, friend.

   b) Give words similar in meaning to:

   lair, disappear, inside, empty, quickly.

3. Give the names of the shops where you would buy the following:

fruit	_____	spectacles	_____	flowers	_____
hats	_____	milk	_____	newspapers	_____
fish	_____	meat	_____	sweets	_____
tobacco	_____				

4. Change all nouns and verbs into plural:
   a)   The lady is very beautiful.
   b)   Is the salmon fresh?
   c)   The son-in-law is ill.
   d)   The valley is broad.
   e)   The goose makes a loud noise.

5. Who use the following articles?

hoe	_____	anvil	_____	safety-lamp	_____
solder	_____	palette	_____	hod	_____
awl	_____	spanner	_____	cleaver	_____

Test 13

1. In the following sentences there are groups of two words within brackets. One of the two words is correct, the other wrong. Underline the correct word:
   a)   William can (ran, run) faster than (I, me).
   b)   It was (me, I) who (did, done) it.
   c)   George and (he, him) (has, have) gone on holiday.
   d)   Between you and (me, I) I think they (was, were) wrong.
   e)   (He, Him) and (me, I) are twelve years of age.

2. A number of sheep is called a flock. Insert the most suitable word in each of the following:
   a)   a _____ of wolves
   b)   a _____ of bees
   c)   a _____ of herring
   d)   a _____ of cattle
   e)   a _____ of ships
   f)   a _____ of singers
   g)   a _____ of thieves

3. In the following sentences underline the correct word of the two words within brackets:
- a) You ought to visit her now (but, that) you know where she stays.
- b) Write down the answers (as, when) you were taught.
- c) The boy tried hard (but, that) he failed.
- d) (Than, When) he comes let us know.
- e) The man was careful (except, lest) he should fall.

4. a) Give the plural of:

deer, mouse, lily, tooth, woman.

b) Give the masculine of:

cow, duchess, duck, actress, niece.

5. By accident the sentences of this story were jumbled. Rearrange them in their proper order:

Fortunately he saved her from serious injury.
Suddenly her ball rolled into the middle of the road, and she ran after it.
A passer-by saw the girl's danger and ran to her aid.
A little girl was playing on a busy street.
At that moment a car came dashing round the corner.

Test 14

1. In the following sentences underline the correct word of the two words within brackets:
- a) How he managed it remains a (duty, mystery).
- b) James was honest and (deceptive, diligent).
- c) The stranger asked if I could (direct, inform) him to the station.
- d) The (remedy, illness) or cure is very simple.
- e) His opinion differed (against, from) mine.

2. a) Punctuate the following correctly:

tell me said the old gentleman what is your name.

b) Form adjectives from:

reason, success, south, fool, France.

3. Use the correct prepositions in the blank spaces:
   a)   The bottle was filled _____ water.
   b)   He was told not to meddle _____ the toys.
   c)   The two brothers divided the apple _____ them.
   d)   That hat is similar _____ mine.
   e)   I hope I can rely _____ you.

4. With whom do you associate the following?
   Example: anvil – blacksmith.
   a)   rifle _____   e)   letters _____
   b)   prescription _____   f)   pulpit _____
   c)   telescope _____   g)   sheep _____
   d)   spectacles _____   h)   joy-stick _____

5. Opposite each phrase are groups of words in brackets. Underline the group of words in brackets which gives the correct meaning of the phrase:

   down in the mouth (speaking quickly) (in low spirits)
   a peppery individual (a quick-tempered person) (a happy person)
   out of sorts (not well) (of great courage)
   hard up (good enough) (short of money)
   beside oneself (annoyed and angry) (nothing to do)

Test 15

1. a)   Underline the correct word of the words in brackets:

   A man who writes stories is an (artist, author, sculptor).
   A bed on board ship is called a (bunk, cabin, saloon).
   A person who hoards money is a (martyr, miser, cashier).
   A vessel for holding flowers is a (caddy, scuttle, vase).
   The flesh of a cow is called (beef, mutton, pork).

  b)   Underline the group of words in brackets which gives the correct meaning of the phrase:

   to play the game (to act fairly) (to run quickly)
   to bury the hatchet (to chop wood) (to make peace)
   to cut a dash (to hurt one's leg) (to be very showy)
   to smell a rat (to be suspicious) (to hunt mice)
   to show the white feather (to be cowardly) (to be proud of an achievement)

2. Underline the correct word of the two words in brackets:

a)   Bernice as well as George (was, were) at the circus.

All of you but Tom (has, have) the wrong answer.

A purse containing three coins (was, were) found.

One and all (is, are) going to the concert.

Neither the one nor the other (is, are) right.

b)   His friend and (he, him) travelled to Paris.

Was it (I, me) you saw there?

Between you and (I, me) I am sure he is wrong.

Emily is younger than (I, me).

Let you and (I, me) hide.

3. a)   Willie has (grew, grown) very tall.

The town crier (rang, rung) his bell.

The boy (began, begun) to look for his pencil.

Has he (wrote, written) to his cousin?

The lion (sprung, sprang) at the timid deer.

b)   The girl wept (bitterly, faintly).

The boy fell (clearly, heavily).

The man crept (harshly, stealthily).

The lady waited (patiently, deeply).

My friend sprang (quickly, plainly).

4. a)   He neither reads (or, nor) writes well.

(Now, When) we arrived we searched for our luggage.

Charles is stronger (as, than) I am.

I know (that, before) Tom is a good scholar.

I could not pay him (that, for) I had no money.

b)   The hunter went in pursuit (to, of) the animal.

He suffers (from, of) a swollen head.

I was sorry to part (of, with) that picture.

The girl complained (with, of) a sore foot.

The man disagreed (of, with) him.

5. a)   In the following lists of words, one word in each list is out of place. Underline this word.

copper, lead, tin, earth, silver.

rain, cold, snow, sleet, hail.

corn, rye, barley, wheat, raisins.

ear, nose, mouth, knee, chin.

linen, leather, silk, cotton, wool.

b)   Underline the word of the same kind as the first three words in each line:
    river, brook, stream (mountain, tributary, island).
    sofa, chair, stool (cupboard, wardrobe, couch).
    limestone, marble, slate (granite, cement, mortar).
    sword, dagger, spear (revolver, rifle, lance).
    kitten, puppy, calf (duck, lamb, horse).

6. Underline the correct word of the two words in brackets:
a)   The ship tied up at the (key, quay).
    He was not (allowed, aloud) to go.
    The jacket was made of (course, coarse) cloth.
    The (pail, pale) moon rose above the hills.
    We picked up shells on the (beach, beech).

b)   Rearrange the following sentences in their proper order so that they form a short story:
    This he did to the great joy of the onlookers.
    He refused to bow to the Governor's hat.
    He ordered him to shoot an apple from his son's head.
    The Governor wished to punish him for his disobedience.
    William Tell was a famous archer in Switzerland.

Test 16

1. Underline the correct word of the group of words in brackets:
a)   A person who eats too much is a (miser, glutton, hypocrite).
b)   A woman who sells vegetables is a (greengrocer, florist, vegetarian).
c)   John, who is my aunt's son, is my (nephew, brother, cousin).
d)   A soldier who rides on horseback is in the (marines, cavalry, infantry).
e)   A wooden shelter made for a dog is a (byre, stable, kennel).

2. Give words opposite in meaning to:

present	_____	bitter	_____
entrance	_____	polite	_____
east	_____	danger	_____
guilty	_____	lost	_____

3. Underline the correct word in each of the brackets:

(Who, Whom) do you think I (saw, seen)?
All but one (was, were) saved when the ship (sank, sunk).
Each of the men (has, have) a right to (their, his) opinion.
Between you and (I, me), the girls (wasn't, weren't) pleased.
Let Maria and (me, I) stay after the others have (gone, went).

4. We say "As black as coal". Supply the missing words in the following:

as blind as	_____	as cold as	_____
as quiet as	_____	as good as	_____
as gentle as	_____	as sharp as	_____
as happy as	_____	as fresh as	_____

5. Following are five sentences, which, if arranged properly, would make a short story. Rearrange them in proper order:

The bird, highly flattered, opened her mouth to sing.
One day a crow spied a piece of cheese on a window sill.
The cheese fell and was soon eaten by the crafty animal.
She picked it up and flew to a neighbouring tree.
A cunning fox approached and praised her voice.

Test 17

1. Christmas Day comes in the month of _____.
Snapper, herring, salmon, bass are all _____.
The masculine of **aunt** is _____.
_____ is the feminine of **hero**.
State the plural of **tooth**.
A number of **sheep** is called a _____.
We say "**As sharp** as a _____".
A person who works on an **anvil** is a _____.
What animal **brays**?
The word for a **young hen** is _____.

2. Give words opposite in meaning to:

defend, stranger, reveal, throw, compliment.

3. The noun formed from **select** is _____.

_____ is the adjective formed from **attract**.

Give a verb corresponding to **broad**.

Form an adverb from **joy**.

Give a compound word with **grand** as part of it.

4. **Bird** is to **air** as **fish** is to _____.

Table is to **wood** as **window** is to _____.

Food is to **hungry** as **drink** is to _____.

Nose is to **smell** as **tongue** is to _____.

Wrist is to **cuff** as **neck** is to _____.

5. In each of the following sentences underline the correct word in brackets:

Many of the pencils were (broke, broken).

Everybody (was, were) pleased with the result.

He is a little taller than (I, me).

The man could not do (nothing, anything) to help.

Neither the boy (or, nor) his sister will come.

To (who, whom) do you wish to speak?

The train moved (slow, slowly) into the station.

The food was pleasant (for, to) the taste.

We received a (strong, hearty) welcome.

Water dripped from the (brim, brink) of his hat.

6. Give words similar in meaning to:

halt, roam, margin, permit, courage.

7. Arrange the following in the correct order, beginning with **dawn**:

dusk, noon, evening, dawn, night, morning.

8. Make short sentences, one for each word, showing the correct use of the following:

their, coarse, fowl, preys, creek.

9. Give **one word** which might be used in place of the words **in bold type**:
a) The prices were **made less than before**.
b) The **people who were listening** applauded.
c) The little boat **turned upside down** in the storm.
d) The germs were **not able to be seen by the human eye**.

10. Name **ten** different **animals**.

Test 18

1. The shortest month of the year is _____.

Cassava, cauliflower, onion and pepper are all _____.

The masculine of **wife** is _____.

_____ is the feminine of **bachelor**.

State the plural of **mouse**.

A number of **thieves** is called a _____.

We say, "As **bold** as_____".

A person who uses a **safety-lamp** is a _____.

What animal **neighs**?

The word for a **young fox** is _____.

2. Give words opposite in meaning to:

arrive, sweet, fertile, legal, juvenile.

3. The noun formed from **young** is _____.

_____ is the adjective formed from **circle**.

Give a verb corresponding to **horror**.

Form an adverb from **weary**.

Give a compound word with **cup** as part of it.

4. Walk is to **legs** as **fly** is to _____.

Knife is to **cut** as **gun** is to _____.

Island is to **sea** as **lake** is to _____.

Statue is to **sculptor** as **book** is to _____.

Petals are to **flower** as **spokes** are to _____.

5. In each of the following sentences underline the correct word in brackets:

A tree had (fell, fallen) across the path.

Neither Tom nor James (is, are) at school.

She is cleverer than (I, me).

He should (of, have) come last night.

Either my father (or, nor) my mother will go with me.

I saw the lad (who, whom) won the race.

It can be done very (easy, easily).

He had not a penny (by, to) his name.

She has a (healthy, spotless) character.

I divided the sweets (between, amongst) several boys.

6. Give words similar in meaning to:

enemy, unite, concluded, guard, envy.

7. Arrange the following in historical order:

   aeroplane, chariot, locomotive, rocket, car.

8. Make short sentences, one for each word, showing the correct use of the following:

   fourth, route, style, soled, sewing.

9. Give **one word** which might be used in place of the words **in bold type**:
   a) Smoking was **not allowed** in the garage.
   b) The motorist drove his car **slowly and carefully**.
   c) The boy **was very sorry for** his mean action.
   d) They ascended the steep steps of the **tower in which the bell was hung**.
   e) The castaways saw a ship on the **line where sea and sky seem to meet**.

10. Name **ten** different **birds**.

Test 19

1. Guy Fawkes' Day is in the month of _____.
   Mosquito, beetle, moth and locust are all _____.
   The masculine of **niece** is _____.
   _____ is the feminine of **wizard**.
   State the plural of **ox**.
   A number of **pupils** is called a _____.
   We say, "As **clear** as _____".
   A person who rides a **bicycle** is called a _____.
   What animal **trumpets**?
   The word for a **young goat** is _____.

2. Give words opposite in meaning to:

   ancient, purchased, private, rare, majority.

3. The noun formed from **choose** is _____.
   _____ is the adjective formed from **voice**.
   Give a verb corresponding to **deed**.
   Form an adverb from **critic**.
   Give a compound word with **ball** as part of it.

4. Picture is to **wall** as carpet is to _____ .

Graceful is to **clumsy** as polite is to _____ .

Descend is to **depth** as ascend is to _____ .

Gas is to **pipes** as electricity is to _____ .

Castle is to **tower** as church is to _____ .

5. In each of the following sentences underline the correct word in brackets:

I have never (went, gone) by bus.

None of the pencils (is, are) missing.

She is much older than (I, me).

We were (learned, taught) how to read correctly.

The boy could neither read (or, nor) write.

(Who, Whom) do you wish to see?

How (quick, quickly) the time has passed!

We waited (upon, for) her at the station.

Between you and (I, me), someone must have taken it.

He divided the apple (between, amongst) his two brothers.

6. Give words similar in meaning to:

vacant, remedy, concealed, grief, faith.

7. Arrange the following in historical order:

canoe, submarine, coracle, steam-ship, sailing-ship.

8. Make short sentences, one for each word, showing the correct use of the following:

waste, aloud, seized, medal, site.

9. Give **one word** which might be used in place of the words **in bold type**:
a)   The boy **purposely kept out of the way of** his employer.
b)   The flowers were **not real, but made of cloth, wax and paper**.
c)   The motor-car **slipped sideways across the road**.
d)   During the fire, the birds had died from **want of air to breathe**.
e)   They managed to fix it with a **sticky substance obtained from the hoofs of animals**.

10. Name **ten** different **flowers**.

Test 20

1. We live in the _____ century.

Coal, iron, slate and lead are all _____.

The masculine of **nun** is _____.

_____ is the feminine of **colt**.

State the plural of **deer**.

A number of **singers** is called a _____.

We say, "As **keen** as _____".

A person who uses a **palette** is an _____.

What animal **howls**?

The word for a **young hare** is _____.

2. Give words opposite in meaning to:

enemy, success, expand, miser, exposed.

3. The noun formed from **receive** is _____.

_____ is the adjective formed from **bible**.

Give a verb corresponding to **grass**.

Form an adverb from **ability**.

Give a compound word with **stone** as part of it.

4. **Sheep** is to **flock** as **tree** is to _____.

Banana is to **peel** as **egg** is to _____.

Speak is to **shout** as **walk** is to _____.

When is to **time** as **where** is to _____.

Lawyer is to **client** as **doctor** is to _____.

5. In each of the following sentences underline the correct word in brackets:

The boy had (rose, risen) at eight o'clock.

Every one of us (has, have) an equal chance.

My sister is five years younger than (I, me).

Do try (to, and) come on time.

Neither a borrower (or, nor) a lender be.

(Who, Whom) do you think we met?

I managed not so (bad, badly).

They were impatient (from, at) the delay.

That is a (trivial, trifling) excuse.

Let Tom and (I, me) go.

6. Give words similar in meaning to:

   commence, repair, odour, prohibited, renown.

7. Arrange the following in historical order:

   oil-lamp, firebrand, electricity, candle, gas.

8. Make short sentences, one for each word, showing the correct use of the following:

   groan, rays, rowed, cruise, cereal.

9. Give **one word** which might be used in place of the words **in bold type**:
   a) The runner was completely **tired and worn out** after the race.
   b) The injured man was **unaware of anything that was going on around him**.
   c) The rude girl continually **broke into** her parents' conversation.
   d) He **changed his appearance by dressing** himself as a native.
   e) The story caused **a state of excited feeling**.

10. Name **ten** different **fruits**.

Tests in Comprehension

Test 1

Read the following passage carefully and then answer the questions below:

The Story of a Great River

From its source in the mountains between Sierra Leone and Guinea to its delta in Eastern Nigeria the mighty Niger will have travelled some 4,000 kilometres. This nine-month-long journey to the far-off Gulf of Guinea will take it through many countries and some of the most varied scenery in the world.

From the high mountains in the Fouta Djallon region through the dense forests of Guinea it flows, gaining in size from its many tributaries. Its waters create the fertile plains of the Mali Republic before reaching the desert regions beyond Timbuktu whence it turns south-eastwards to flow between the republics of Niger and Benin.

It is here that it enters Nigeria, that great African state and, more than half its journey over, is put to work. Vast hydro-electric plants provide for the needs of Nigeria's millions and for the industry of this huge country. Here, too, irrigation schemes, fed by its waters, assist in food production and its use, with specially designed vessels, to facilitate travel, trade and the transport of goods. And everywhere there are fishermen casting their nets.

At Lokoja, where the Niger is joined by its greatest tributary, the Benue, it turns sharply southwards to flow majestically past Onitsha and presently to form its vast delta. This delta, hot and humid, is a place of great rainforests, mangrove swamps and a network of waterways taking the Niger at last to the sea. Here, too, and in the sea offshore, are the oil-fields which make Nigeria one of the main oil producers of the Commonwealth of Nations.

Marks

1. Where is the source of the Niger? (1)
2. Name three towns on its banks. (2)
3. Through which countries does it pass? (1)
4. In which country is its delta? (1)
5. In your own words describe a delta. (3)
6. In your own words describe a mangrove. (2)
7. What is opposite in direction to south-east? (2)
8. What confluence occurs at Lokoja? (2)
9. Find out and write about Mungo Park. (5)
10. Write short notes on the following:
    Hausa, Yoruba, lbo, Fulani, Tiv, Kanuri. (6)

Total 25

Test 2

Read the following passage carefully and then answer the questions below:

Homework Interrupted

Tabu looked up from his book, in a lazy way at first, to see what had made the noise. Then he went stiff with fright. At an arm's length away from his chair, something moved. A shape glided smoothly along the window frame. He saw a flat head held up by a slender neck. A puff adder!

The snake stopped and lay without moving. It looked dead. But all the time it was trying to sense if any food was in the room.

Tabu felt trapped in his chair, yet he knew he must warn his sister. He thought of what his father had told him so often. He wanted to whisper, but his mouth and tongue were dry with shock. He dared not move. His throat clicked as he tried to utter some sound. If only she would look at him!

Masya must have felt that there was something strange about his silence, for she turned her head to glance at him. When she saw the fear on his face, she swiftly shifted round, looking at his glazed eyes. She moved her head to see what those eyes were fixed on, then covered her mouth to stifle her gasp of terror.

(From *World Wide Adventure Series* Reader 5 – published by Robert Gibson.)

Marks

1. What had the snake come for? (1)
2. Why would it stop and lie without moving? (1)
3. What made Tabu feel trapped in his chair? (2)
4. What effects did Tabu's fear have on him? (2)
5. Why would he wish to warn his sister? (2)
6. What do you think Tabu's father had told him so often? (2)
7. What caused Masya to look at Tabu? (1)
8. How did she come to see where the danger was? (1)
9. Why did she cover her mouth? (2)
10. What might have happened if Tabu had moved? (2)
11. What do you think Tabu wanted to warn his sister to do or not to do? (4)
12. What would you have done in Tabu's place? (5)

Total 25

Test 3

Read the following passage carefully and then answer the questions below:

The Fox

The fox is probably the most intelligent of all quadrupeds. It is allied to the dog and closely resembles the Alsatian, the wolf, the hyena, the coyote (prairie-wolf of North America), the dingo (native dog of Australia), and the dhole (wild dog of India). Its chief points of difference from the others are the sharper muzzle and the shorter legs in proportion to the size of the body. Its tail or "brush" is also longer, and its ears more erect.

The fox has eyes with pupils that contract in strong light and expand in darkness. This enables the animal to hunt at night. It excavates its own lair by burrowing much like a rabbit, but frequently it is a thief in this respect as it steals burrows from other animals and converts them into its own "earth". The cunning and slyness of the animal is shown by the number of exits to its lair. As many as ten bolt-holes from the fox's "earth" have been counted. Its power of scent is very acute, and its hearing very highly developed. The animal has a peculiar strong scent, which leaves the "trail" in the so-called sport of fox-hunting. When the chase is keen Reynard frequently escapes by dashing into wide and open drainpipes. For this reason one may see gratings placed over the mouths of many roadside and field drains. When cornered by the hounds the animal has been known to climb roofs of houses and to dash into nearby cottages in desperate efforts to shake off its pursuers.

Marks

1. What is a quadruped? (1)
2. Name ten animals mentioned in the passage. (5)
3. Give four points of difference between the fox and the dog. (4)
4. Why is the fox able to hunt at night? (1)
5. Name any other creature which hunts at night. (1)
6. What two words are used for the fox's den? (2)
7. Of what use are bolt-holes? (1)
8. What animal does the fox resemble when digging? (1)
9. Give two reasons why the fox is a difficult animal to catch. (2)
10. What enables the hounds to track down the fox? (1)
11. What special name is sometimes given to a fox? (1)
12. According to the passage, why do gratings sometimes cover drainpipes? (1)
13. What is meant by "When the chase is keen"? (1)
14. Give the meanings of the following words as used in the passage:
    contract, excavates, frequently, converts, scent, peculiar. (3)

Total 25

Test 4

Read the following passage (supposed to have been written by a boy) and then answer the questions below:

> When I had finished breakfast the squire gave me a note addressed to John Silver, at the sign of the Spy-glass, and told me I should easily find the place by following the line of the docks, and keeping a bright look-out for a little tavern with a large brass telescope for sign. I set off, overjoyed at this opportunity to see some more of the ships and seamen, and picked my way among a great crowd of people and carts and bales, for the dock was now at its busiest, until I found the tavern in question. It was a bright enough little place of entertainment. The sign was newly painted; the windows had neat red curtains; the floor was newly sanded. There was a street on either side, and an open door on both, which made the large, low room pretty clear to see in, in spite of clouds of tobacco smoke. The customers were mostly sea-faring men; and they talked so loudly that I hung at the door, almost afraid to enter. As I was waiting, a man came out of a side room, and, at a glance, I was sure he must be Long John. His left leg was cut off close by the hip, and under the left shoulder he carried a crutch, which he managed with wonderful dexterity. He seemed in the most cheerful spirits, whistling as he moved about among the tables.

Marks

1. To whom was the squire's note addressed? (1)
2. Where was this person to be found? (1)
3. At what time of day did the boy set out? (1)
4. What route was he to take? (1)
5. Why was the boy overjoyed? (2)
6. When the boy had found the tavern in question, what did he notice about
   a) the sign, b) the windows, c) the floor? (3)
7. Who were the customers? (1)
8. Why was the boy almost afraid to enter? (2)
9. Where was John Silver when the boy first looked into the tavern? (1)
10. What nickname is used in the passage? (2)
11. Describe John Silver's unusual appearance. (4)
12. How do you know Silver was happy? (1)
13. Give another word of the same meaning for each of the following:
    spy-glass, tavern, opportunity, glance, dexterity. (5)

Total 25

Test 5

Read the following passage carefully and then answer the questions below:

Sightseeing in Singapore

You do not have to go far in Singapore to discover the unexpected or the unusual. A stroll through Chinatown could bring you face to face with a cartful of masks for people to wear to represent mythical or historical characters in a procession or an operatic or theatrical performance during some festival – heads of heroes and villains, horses and lions, unicorns and dragons, all crafted with loving care and selling at surprisingly low prices. Go and listen to the early morning "concert" of birdsong from hundreds of caged birds. Have your initials carved in semi-precious stone to make your own personal seal. Notice the old women working on a construction site, clad in black and wearing red head-dresses. These are the Samsui sisters who have voluntarily chosen to adopt this way of life and remain unmarried.

The variety of things to do in Singapore is endless. Relax on a tropical beach, take a stroll through a lush green park or visit an Indian temple. You can spend hours in the Zoological Gardens with their world-famous Orang-utan colony, spot 350 different species among the 7,000 birds in the Bird Park, see the Orchid Garden with its thousands of blooms that would cost a king's ransom in London, or visit a crocodile farm.

After your sightseeing you may be hungry, and there is no better place to be hungry than in Singapore. Rich aromas will draw you to one of Singapore's 8,000 open-air food-stalls offering Chinese, Malay, and Indian dishes in all their infinite variety – with a banana leaf, perhaps, to serve as your plate and end the day with yet another surprise.

(*Information Source:* Singapore Tourist Promotion Board.)

Marks

1. What is a *mythical* character? (2)
2. How is a *historical* character different? (2)
3. How do *operatic* and *theatrical* productions differ? (2)
4. What does *crafted* mean? Why is it a good word here? (2)
5. Why would the low prices be surprising? (2)
6. Why is the word "concert" in inverted commas? (2)
7. What would be the purpose of having a personal seal? (2)
8. What is a construction site? (2)
9. What does the word *species* mean? What is its singular? (2)
10. What does *a king's ransom* mean and why? (2)
11. What would be the purpose of a crocodile farm? (2)
12. Distinguish *flavours*, *aromas*, *smells* and *perfumes*. (3)

Total 25

Test 6

Read the following passage carefully and then answer the questions below:

The Long Trek

Steve reckoned that they were about three miles from the river, if there was still a river. By now, it might be just a trickle of slow-moving water, or a bed of dried mud, full of tumbleweed and stones.

He closed his eyes to slits as he peered through the clouds of dust – red dust kicked up by hundreds of hoofs. The cattle that streamed past him as he sat slumped in his saddle were as tired and worn out as the exhausted men who drove them.

Some of them bellowed with fear and pain. The calves pushed their noses into the sides of the cows that had no more milk to feed them. All of them were mad with thirst and very thin. From their knob-like backbones, the drawn skin was tight over the fleshless haunches. Their ribs curved like the bars of a cage over their sunken flanks. They were starving.

They had trekked from the cattle stations in the north of Australia where usually heavy rains filled streams and pools. But this was a year of drought. The burning sun, which had sucked up the last drops of water, had left the ground cracked and dry. Wide, dangerous ruts had formed in the earth. They were deep and broad enough to wedge a man's boot when he walked. There was only one thing to do. The cattle must be driven many miles south, to the river; or they would die.

(From *World Wide Adventure Series* Reader 5 – published by Robert Gibson.)

	Marks
1. Why did Steve sit "slumped" in his saddle?	(2)
2. What did he fear might have happened to the river?	(3)
3. Why were the animals' backbones like knobs?	(1)
4. What other effects had the drought had on them?	(3)
5. What is a drought?	(1)
6. Why would the ground have cracks?	(2)
7. Had the sun really "sucked" up drops of water?	(3)
8. Why were the ruts in the earth dangerous?	(1)
9. If the river was dry, what then?	(4)
10. What effects would a drought have in your area?	(5)
	Total 25

Test 7

Read over the following passage and then answer the questions below:

The Death of James I of Scotland

The king, while he was staying at Perth, took up his residence in the abbey of Black Friars, there being no convenient palace in the town, and this made it easier for his enemies to carry out their purpose, as his guards and officers were staying in different houses.

Just as James, having dismissed all his attendants, was preparing to go to bed, the Highland woman who had already warned him at the ferry again demanded permission to speak with the king, but was refused on account of the lateness of the hour. Suddenly a clashing of armour was heard in the garden and flashes of light from torches were thrown against the windows. The king, hearing the voice of Sir Robert Graham, his deadly enemy, guessed that the intruders had come to murder him. He called to the ladies to keep the door as well as they could, while he tried to get out at the windows, but the bars would not budge. By the help of tongs, however, he lifted a plank of the flooring, and let himself down into a narrow vault beneath. This vault had formerly had an opening into the courtyard of the convent, by which he might have made his escape, but the unfortunate James forgot that, only three days before, he had caused the opening to be built up, because when he played at ball in the courtyard the ball used to roll into the vault through that hole.

The queen and her women endeavoured as well as they might to keep the door shut, and one of them, Katherine Douglas, boldly thrust her arm across the door in place of the bar, which the conspirators had removed the day before.

	Marks
1. Why did the king stay in an abbey at Perth?	(1)
2. Why did the king's enemies find it easy to attack him in the abbey?	(1)
3. Why did the woman want to speak with the king?	(2)
4. Why was the Highland woman turned from the door?	(1)
5. What two things alarmed the king and the ladies?	(2)
6. Why did the king fear the intruders?	(2)
7. Why could James not jump from a window?	(1)
8. How did the king escape from the room?	(1)
9. When the king let himself into the vault what did he expect to do?	(2)
10. Why had the vault entrance been closed?	(2)
11. How had the conspirators prepared, the day before, for the murder?	(2)
12. Describe a "torch" of the time of this story.	(2)
13. Give another word with the same meaning for each of the following: residence, convenient, budge, unfortunate, endeavoured, conspirators.	(6)

Total 25

Test 8

Read this passage carefully and then answer the questions below:

Shipwreck on a Coral Island

A huge wave snatched up the oar that we had decided to cling to instead of joining the ship's crowded boat, and . . .

I came to on the shore to find young Peterkin trying to staunch the flow of blood from my badly cut brow, and learned from Jack that we appeared to be the only survivors, alone on an uninhabited island.

It soon occurred to Peterkin, the youngest of us at fourteen, that hunger and thirst might be a problem. The ship's stores were sunk in deep water. What would we do? Jack pointed up to the branched head of a coconut palm. "There, look!" he said, "Nuts at all stages."

In no time Peterkin had monkeyed up and tossed down three nuts about the size of a football.

"Let's visit the wreck first," said Jack, "and then eat."

Though only eighteen himself, Jack was our natural leader and no one objected, Peterkin comforting himself by telling us that he'd rather find a spring, and have a drink, than eat.

"Then hop up that tree again," said Jack, "and throw down another nut, a green one this time, unripe."

Surprised, but always game, Peterkin did as he was told.

"Now cut a hole in it with your knife and clap it to your mouth."

Peterkin did as directed, and we both burst into uncontrolled laughter at the changes that instantly passed over his face. No sooner had he put the nut to his mouth and thrown back his head to catch what came out, than his eyes opened to twice their ordinary size, while his throat moved vigorously in the act of swallowing. Then a look of intense delight spread over his face except, of course, his mouth, which was otherwise engaged. At length he stopped, drew a long breath, and exclaimed, "Nectar! Perfect nectar!"

(Adapted from *The Coral Island* by R. M. Ballantyne.)

Marks

1. What happened between the first and second paragraphs? (2)
2. How are we expected to know this? (2)
3. Why is *staunch* a better word than *stop* (paragraph 2)? (2)
4. What did Jack mean by "nuts at all stages"? (2)
5. What do the words *monkeyed* and *hop* suggest? (2)
6. Why could they not get food from the wreck? (2)
7. Why did Jack first speak of eating but not drinking? (2)
8. Which sentences show Jack as a good leader? (2)
9. Is *objecting* different from *refusing*? (2)
10. Why did the others laugh at Peterkin? (2)
11. What feelings can make us wide-eyed? (2)
12. What does "otherwise engaged" mean? (1)
13. What was the point of exclaiming "Nectar!"? (2)

Total 25

Test 9

Read this passage carefully and then answer the questions below:

Nature and the Traveller in the Caribbean

Nature shows off to the traveller in the Caribbean. Start in the Cayman Islands and she introduces you to some of her prize travellers, the turtles that swim thousands of miles to these sandy shores to lay their eggs.

Watch Neptune's gliders, the "flying" fish, skimming the tips of waves as you make for Jamaica and sail into one of the world's great natural harbours. Go ashore and see huge crawling monsters clawing out mountains of bauxite from which will come aluminium, "silver from clay", to be made into kitchen utensils and tomorrow's jumbo jets.

Don't miss seeing the phenomenal lush growth of a tropical rainforest, on Dominica, where the tree canopy blots out the sun.

On Barbados stand and watch the Atlantic's majestic rollers crashing against the foot of the island's northern rock-face, tossing up spray twice the height of the cliffs. There too you will marvel, as elsewhere, at the unimaginable number of tiny coral insects that had to live and die to form these miles of bright clean sands, reefs and whole coral islands.

Drive over the wild moon landscape of the crater of St Lucia's Soufrière volcano, its deafening jets of steam showing it is not yet dead, only sleeping. Then take your pictures, as everyone does, of the island's twin sugar-loaf mountains rising 800 metres sheer out of the sea, and move on, perhaps flying over the volcanoes of St Vincent and Grenada, their craters now occupied by lakes, to busy Trinidad. Here see the pitch lake Sir Walter Raleigh used to waterproof his ships' hulls, and which today, after four hundred years, still supplies asphalt for our roads.

And these ships in the bay? Nature will fill them again and again with the oil she has made from the remains of living things that lived here long before history.

Now step over to South America and see one final marvel, Guyana's Kaieteur Falls, five times the height of Niagara, a spectacular end to an unforgettable trip.

Marks

1. Does nature "show off"? What is meant? (2)
2. In what way are the turtles "prize travellers"? (2)
3. Does the writer think flying fish really fly? (2)
4. What "crawling monster" would you see in Jamaica? (2)
5. Why is aluminium called "silver from clay"? (2)
6. What makes the forests on Dominica so lush? (2)
7. Compare *rollers* with other words that could be used. (2)
8. How are coral reefs formed? (2)
9. What do the words *moon landscape* suggest? (2)
10. Is it better to call the volcano *sleeping* than *dormant*? (2)
11. Explain the second last paragraph. (3)
12. What makes things *spectacular*? (2)

Total 25

Test 10

Read this passage carefully and then answer the questions below:

Monday Morning

Monday morning found Tom Sawyer miserable. Monday morning always found him so, because it began another week's slow suffering in school. He generally began that day with wishing he had had no intervening holiday; it made the going into captivity and fetters again so much more odious.

Tom lay thinking. Presently it occurred to him that he wished he was sick; then he could stay at home from school. Here was a vague possibility. He canvassed his system. No ailment was found, and he investigated again. This time he thought he could detect colicky symptoms, and he began to encourage them with considerable hope. But they soon grew feeble and presently died wholly away. He reflected further. Suddenly he discovered something. One of his upper teeth was loose. This was lucky; he was about to groan, as a "starter", as he called it, when it occurred to him that if he came into court with that argument his aunt would pull it out, and that would hurt. So he thought he would hold the tooth in reserve for the present, and seek further. Nothing offered for some little time, and then he remembered hearing the doctor tell about a certain thing that laid up a patient for two or three weeks and threatened to make him lose a finger. So the boy eagerly drew his sore toe from under the sheet and held it up for inspection. But now he did not know the necessary symptoms. However, it seemed well worthwhile to chance it, so he fell to groaning with considerable spirit.

Mark Twain

Marks

1. Where was Tom when he was doing his thinking? (1)
2. What prospect was making him miserable? (1)
3. What made the misery worse on Mondays? (1)
4. What was the purpose of his thinking? (1)
5. What three ideas did he have for achieving his purpose? (3)
6. What caused him to reject his first idea? (1)
7. How do we know he thought the second idea was better? (1)
8. Why did he not adopt this second idea? (1)
9. How did he set about carrying out his third plan? (1)
10. What weakness can you see in this third plan? (1)
11. In what sense was Tom facing captivity and fetters? (1)
12. What is meant by the words "canvass" (compare "canvas") and "system"? (2)
13. What would Tom do in "canvassing his system"? (2)
14. In the phrase "came into court with that argument" what court is meant, and what argument? (2)
15. What is meant by holding the tooth "in reserve"? (1)
16. What is the difference between a symptom and an ailment? (2)
17. Which words used in the passage refer to *feelings*, and which other words refer to *thinking*? (3)

Total 25

Test 11

Read this passage carefully and then answer the questions which follow:

Africa is the second largest continent and is a land of great contrasts. It has burning deserts and luxurious forests teeming with animal life.

North of the Sahara Desert on the Mediterranean coast are the Arab States, to the South are the ex-colonies, now self-governing. Europe is only 9 miles from the North African coast at the Straits of Gibraltar. To the North East, in Egypt, the Suez Isthmus joins Africa to Asia. The Isthmus is cut by the 72-mile stretch of the Suez Canal which provides passage for ships from the Indian Ocean to the Mediterranean Sea and the Atlantic Ocean.

The equator passes through the centre of Africa at Mount Kenya, and most of the continent lies in the Tropics, i.e. between the tropic of Cancer and the tropic of Capricorn.

Because of Africa's smooth coastline there are few inlets and bays.

The largest island is the Republic of Madagascar in the Indian Ocean. The Cape Verde Islands, the Canaries, and Madeira are all groups of islands off the North West coast.

Most of the land is one vast plateau. There is only a narrow coastal plain in most places but this broadens in the North East and North West. The plateau is stepped, and on each "step" there are wide, flat tracts of land with few mountains.

One remarkable feature of the geography of the continent, and indeed of the world, is the Great Rift Valley, formed where the land has sunk between two faults in the Earth's crust. One branch of this rift is occupied by Lake Albert, Lake Tanganyika, Lake Nyasa and the last 200 miles of the course of the Zambesi River. The other branch runs through Kenya from Lake Nyasa and is occupied by the Red Sea in the North, continuing up the Gulf of Aqaba and the valley of the River Jordan in Asia.

There are three great deserts which form two fifths of the continental area, the Sahara in the North (the largest in area) the Kalahari in the South and the Namib along the South West coast.

The highest mountain is Kilimanjaro, with its 19,340 feet (5895 metre) Uhuru Peak, which is always snow-covered though almost on the equator. This and other mountains are volcanic in origin and a few volcanoes are still active. The Atlas mountains cut off the Sahara from the western Mediterranean and the Atlantic. The second largest fresh-water lake in the world, Lake Victoria, lies between the two arms of the Rift Valley.

Africa's rivers include some of the longest in the world. The Nile drains huge areas from the equator to the Mediterranean, providing Egypt with rich silt for crops and water to irrigate them. The Congo Basin is one of the world's great tropical rainforests. The Niger probably waters more countries than any other river. The Zambesi boasts the world's greatest waterfalls and, like the Volta, has been put to work to provide millions with electricity.

1. The passage is about:
   A. *the Sahara Desert*
   B. *the geography of Africa*
   C. *the African coastline*
   D. *the tropic of Capricorn.*

2. Which of these has nothing to do with the passage?
   A. *Madagascar*
   B. *drilling for oil*
   C. *the Sahara Desert*
   D. *the Indian Ocean.*

3. From the passage we learn:
   A. *Africa is the second largest continent*
   B. *Africa is a winter resort of migrant birds*
   C. *Africa is moving slowly (drifting)*
   D. *Africa has four deserts.*

4. According to the passage, Africa is:
   A. *one vast plateau*
   B. *full of active volcanoes*
   C. *surrounded by islands*
   D. *made up of jungle.*

5. The Atlas mountains
   A. *lie beside the Mediterranean*
   B. *meet the Indian Ocean*
   C. *join Egypt at the Suez Canal*
   D. *cut off the Sahara from the western Mediterranean.*

6. From the passage we can conclude:
   A. *Africa has a rocky coastline*
   B. *Africa is surrounded on three sides by oceans*
   C. *it is possible to sail right round Africa*
   D. *snow is unknown in Kenya.*

7. The largest island, or group of islands, off the African coast is:
   A. *Madeira*
   B. *Canaries*
   C. *the Cape Verde Islands*
   D. *Madagascar.*

8. There is a narrow coastal plain:
   A. *to the North around the Atlas mountains*
   B. *south of the Equator*
   C. *to the South West at the Namib Desert*
   D. *in most places.*

9. From the passage we learn that the Great Rift Valley was formed by
   A. *erosion due to weather*
   B. *volcanic eruptions*
   C. *sinking of the land between cracks in the earth's crust*
   D. *rivers gouging out a channel for themselves.*

10. From the passage, which of these is not a feature of African geography?
   A. *the Kalahari Desert*
   B. *ships in the Suez Canal*
   C. *the smooth coastline*
   D. *the great plateau.*

11. Where does the Mediterranean meet the Atlantic?
   A. *at Madagascar*
   B. *at Lake Victoria*
   C. *at the Strait of Gibraltar*
   D. *near the Sahara Desert.*

Standard English Pronunciation

Unless you pronounce your words correctly giving the vowels and consonants their correct value, the sounds which you make will not be understood. In this chapter we set out most of the variety of sounds used in speaking English, give you practice in these sounds and identify, and help you to avoid, the common errors of speech. Throughout this chapter, where further practice is considered desirable, reference has been made to the lists of words in *Sounds of Words* Books 1 or 2 (published by Hodder Gibson).

We will start with the simple single vowel sounds and proceed by easy stages to cover and give practice in all the necessary sounds. Remember to practise the starters until you sound perfect before going on to complete words.

Some '*a*' sounds

Practise starters *ma', pa', ra', ca', fa'*.
ma'n, pa'n, ra'n, ca'n, fa'n, Dan, Sam, Pam, tan, yam.
(For further practice SOW Book 1, pages 7 & 8.)

Some '*e*' sounds

Practise starters *be', le', ke', pe', te'*.
be'g, le'g, ke'g, pe'g, Te'd, bed, led, fed, sell, fell.
(For further practice SOW Book 1, pages 11 & 12.)

Some '*i*' sounds

Practise starters *wi', ki', i', bi'*.
wi'll, wi'n, ki'd, li'd, bi'll, lip, sip, pick, sick, wick.
(For further practice SOW Book 1, pages 15 & 16.)

Some '*o*' sounds

Practise starters *fo', no', lo', so'*.
fo'g, no'd, lo'g, no't, so'p, bog, cot, dog, for, got.
(For further practice SOW Book 1, page 19.)

Some '*u*' sounds

Practise starters *gu', bu', cu', du'*.
gu'n, gu'm, bu'n, cu't, du'll, bus, cup, fur, hurt, just.
(For further practice SOW Book 1, pages 21 & 22.)

Revision

it, pat, pig, us, van, mat, jug, bed, lad, met, mutt, tan, led, yam, cup, dog, Meg, hog, hug, sip.

For further revision in the sounds you have just learned, turn to SOW Book 1, page 23.

'*ck*'

Remember to prolong the vowel and emphasise the final '*ck*'.

Practise starters *ba*', *ne*', *ti*', *to*', *su*'.

ba'ck, ne'ck, ti'ck, to'ck, su'ck, lack, peck, sick, lock, luck.

(For further practice SOW Book 1, page 25.)

Emphasise the final consonants

damp, send, kept, pack, rust, went, sand, text, rack, pump.

(For further practice SOW Book 1, pages 27, 28, 29, 30.)

Get the 'starters' correct

bla'ck, cri'sp, sti'ck, tra'mp, sta'ck, dre'ss, dru'm, lucky, sorry, fuzzy.

(For further practice SOW Book 1, pages 32, 33, 35.)

The missing '*e*'

The final '*e*' is not pronounced in certain words.

candle, dazzle, paddle, fizzle, battle, cattle, kettle, puddle.

(For further practice SOW Book 1, page 39.)

The '*sh*' sound

Practise the '*sh*' 'starters' *sha*', *she*', *shi*', *sho*', *shu*'.

shirt, shop, sham, shell, shed, shut, shock, shot, short, shod.

(For further practice SOW Book 1, page 41.)

Note that '*sh*' at the end of the words has the same sound.

fish, dish, crush, crash.

(For further practice SOW Book 1, page 42.)

The '*th*' sounds

Practise the '*th*' starters and endings.

thumb, cloth, wrath, lath, that, thong, thing, them, bath.

(For further practice SOW Book 1, pages 43 & 44.)

The '*ch*' sound

Practise the starters and endings.

chick, church, match, branch, latch, batch, chap, chip, check.

(For further practice SOW Book 1, pages 45 & 46.)

The '*wh*' sound

Practise the starters *whi*', *wha*', *whe*'.

whi'p, whi'sk, whi'stle, wha't, when, where, whit, whack, whiz, whim.

(For further practice SOW Book 1, pages 47 & 48.)

The 'ng' sound

wing, bang, sting, hang, sang, rang, long, rung.
(For further practice SOW Book 1, page 50.)

a – e

The silent 'e' changes the 'a' sound.
The silent 'e' makes 'a' as in *man*, sound *ā* as in *day*, *hay*, *lay*.
ba'ke, ba'se, ha're, ta'ble, case, lake, make, cake.
(For further practice SOW Book 2, pages 4 & 5.)

i – e

The silent 'e' changes the 'i' sound.
The silent 'e' changes the 'i' as in *lip*, *pip* to 'i' as in *fire*.
Practise starters *fi'*, *mi'*, *pi'*, *li'*, *hi'*.
fire, mine, pipe, like, hide, dice, white.
(For further practice SOW Book 2, pages 6 & 7.)

o – e

The silent 'e' changes the 'o' sound as in *rod* to the 'o' as in *rode*.
nose, toes, roes, goes, prose, floes, notes, mote, rote.
(For further practice SOW Book 2, pages 8 & 9.)

u – e

The silent 'e' changes the 'u' sound as in *tub*, *rub* to the 'u' as in *tube*.
cube, tune, cure, use, rude, pure, glue, blue, true.

'y'

The 'y' sounds like 'i'.
Practise the 'y' sound – fly, sky, try, dry, fry, cry, shy, by, my.

'i'

Practise this new 'i' sound.
tie, die, died, cried, fried, tried, spied, shied.

'i' Another sound

child, wild, mild, kind, hind, mind, blind, find, bind, rind.

Revision *a – e*, *i – e*, *o – e*, *u – e*, *y*, *i*.

Remember to sound your starters and go over the sounds you have just learned.
Remind yourself of the various similar 'y' and 'i' sounds.
(For further revision SOW Book 2, pages 12 & 13.)

'ay' , 'ai'

'ay' as in *play* and *hay* sounds the same as 'ai' in *rain* and *sail*.
tray, may, say, pail, mail, day, Kay, jay, pray, wait.
(For further practice SOW Book 2, pages 14 & 15.)

'ee'

'ee' as in *see, wee, wheel, week*

seek, leek, feel, heel, keep, meet, peek, reek, seek, deer, jeer, seer.

(For further practice SOW Book 2, pages 16 & 17.)

'ea'

'ea' as in *ear* and *eat* sounds the same as the 'ee' sound.

pea, sea, lea, dear, tear, fear, gear, hear, near, rear.

(For further practice SOW Book 2, pages 18 & 19.)

'qu' = kw

'qu' as in *queen, squeak, quack*.

quads, quail, quake, quart, quench, quick, quest, quiet, quit, quiz.

'oo'

'oo' as in *soot, rook, book* requires considerable practice in the starters *roo', boo', too', coo'*.

rook, pool, took, tool, hook, cook, nook.

(For further practice SOW Book 2, pages 22 & 23.)

'ow' 'ou'   (Two similar sounds)

'ow' as in *now*.

how, brown, bow, dower, power, row, sow, tower.

'ou' as in *out*.

flour, found, shout, ouch, sound, round.

(For further practice SOW Book 2, pages 24 & 25.)

'wa' 'aw' 'all'

'wa' as in *warm* is a similar sound to 'aw' as in *saw*: and the 'a' in *all* says 'aw' as in *ball*.

'wa' as in *wad*.

waddle, waffle, walk, wallet, walrus, waltz, war, ward, warn, wash.

'aw' as in *awful*.

awning, awkward, bawl, dawn, dawdle, fawn, hawk, lawn.

'all' as in *tall*.

stall, ball, call, fall, gall, hall, mall, wall.

(For further practice SOW Book 2, pages 26 & 27.)

'oa'

The 'oa' sound is that of a long 'o' as in *loaf*.

goat, goal, oak, soak, oar, oats, boat, coat, coast, foam, goal, hoax.

(For further practice SOW Book 2, pages 28 & 29.)

'ow'

The 'ow' sound, usually at the end of a word, is that of a long 'o' as in *slow*.

below, arrow, sparrow, barrow, harrow, narrow, stow, row, crow, throw, lower, snow.

(For further practice SOW Book 2, pages 30 & 31.)

'ce' = s

The 'ce' sound is that of 's' as in *mice*.

lace, voice, face, choice, dice, cedar, cease, dance, lance, glance.

(For further practice SOW Book 2, pages 32 & 33.)

'ge' = j

The 'ge' sound is that of 'j' as in *rage*.

cage, hinge, gem, gender, general, gentle, sage, savage, lunge, manage, strange.

(For further practice SOW Book 2, page 34.)

Revision

Go back to the 'ai', 'ay' sounds and, doing a few starters, say aloud five of each sound up to 'ge'.

(Further revision SOW Book 2, page 35.)

The silent 'k'

'k' before 'n' is silent as in *knot*.

knee, knife, knock, kneel, knot, knob, know, knoll, knell.

(For further practice SOW Book 2, page 36.)

The silent 'w'

'w' before 'r' is silent as in *wreck*.

wrong, wrap, write, wretch, wren, writhe, wrath, wring, wristlet, wrench, wrestle.

(For further practice SOW Book 2, page 37.)

The silent 'b'

lamb, thumb, dumb, numb, crumb, bomb, comb, climb.

(For further practice SOW Book 2, page 38.)

The silent 't'

whistle, castle, wrestle, bustle, rustle, listen, often, soften, glisten, hustle.

(For further practice SOW Book 2, page 38.)

Spelling Guide

Advice

Remember the appearance of difficult words you meet in books.

Your mind's eye is a great aid to good spelling and will often tell you what is right (or wrong).

Consult your dictionary if in any doubt.

Pronounce words correctly when you speak. For example:

Pronounce the *r* after the *b* in *February*.
Pronounce the *g* in *recognise*.
Pronounce *secretary* as four syllables, and so on.
Your ear will then help you to avoid many mistakes.

Though English spelling refuses to be bound by rules, some rules are worth studying for the help they can give.

i before *e*, except after *c*

The rule is only partly true, but can be improved thus:
'If sounded as *ee*, then *i* before *e*, except after *c*.

If they sound *ay* or *eye*, then *e* before *i*.'

This table shows the variety of cases:

Sounded as:	Spelling	Examples and Exceptions
ee in *see*	*ie*	belief, cashier, chief, hygiene, grieve, siege.
		Exceptions: protein, seize, weir, weird, and personal names like Neil, Reith, Sheila.
i in *bit*	*ie*	sieve, mischief, mischievous, handkerchief.
		Exceptions: foreign, forfeit, surfeit.
ee in *see* (after *c*)	*ei*	ceiling, conceive, deceit, perceive, receipt.
		Exceptions: specie, species (and see below).
ay in *day*	*ei*	eight, neighbour, reign, sovereign, weigh.
ey in *eye*	*ei*	eiderdown, either, height, neither, sleight.
e in *met*	*ei*	heifer, leisure.
		Exceptions: friend, lieutenant.
separate	*i + e*	diet, glazier, soviet, science.
separate	*e + i*	deity, homogeneity.

Note: *ie* is found after *c* where *ci* sounds *sh* in:
ancient, conscience, deficient, efficient, proficient, sufficient.

Plurals of Nouns

English nouns have a great variety of plural forms – one result of inheriting and borrowing from many languages:

-s   added to the singular – by far the most common form.
> bats, bones, days, keys, chiefs, pianos.

-es   added to the singular where the singular ends in -s or another sibilant (hiss) sound, -ss, -x, -sh, -ch.
> asses, lynxes, wishes, torches, lunches.

-s   is added to most singulars ending in -o but -es to some, and either -s or es to others.

> **-s**   for Italian, Spanish, art, musical terms, abbreviations
>> pianos, altos, sopranos, sombreros, photos.

> **-s**   for singulars ending in two vowels
>> shampoos, studios, patios, kangaroos, videos.

> **-es**   buffaloes, dominoes, mosquitoes, tomatoes, volcanoes.

> **-s** or **-es** flamingo(e)s, motto(e)s, stiletto(e)s.

-ies   replaces -y, but **not** -ay, -ey, -oy, or -uy of singulars.
> allies, berries, copies, hobbies, tries, varieties.

-ves   replaces -f or -fe of the singular in a few words.
> elves, shelves, sheaves, wives.

-x   is added to the singular – beaux, bureaux (from French).

-i   replaces -us as in fungus, fungi; radius, radii (Latin).

-a   replaces -um as in stratum, strata; datum, data (Latin).

-ices   replaces -ex as in index, indices (Latin).

-es   replaces -is as in axis, axes; basis, bases (Greek).

-a   replaces -on as in criteria, phenomena (Greek).

See also page 2 for plurals formed by changing a vowel, nouns with two plurals, plurals the same as singulars, nouns which have no singular, and for further examples.

Spelling Words with Suffixes

We add suffixes to words for a variety of purposes – for example, to make plurals, to make adjectives from nouns, adverbs from adjectives, etc. See pages 2, 72 to 75, 117 to 120.

Quite often the spelling of a base word is changed when a suffix is added. In almost every case it is the last letter of the base word that is affected.

For example:

Final *y* becomes *i*   easy+ly becomes eas<u>i</u>ly.

Final *e* is dropped   hope+ing becomes ho<u>p</u>ing.

Final consonant doubled   hop+ing becomes hop<u>p</u>ing.

Final -*y*

Final -*y* after consonants usually becomes *i* (*ie* before *s*)

den<u>y</u>, deni<u>e</u>-s, den<u>i</u>-ed, den<u>i</u>-al; luxury, luxur<u>i</u>ous;

beaut<u>y</u>, beaut<u>i</u>ful; marr<u>y</u>, marr<u>i</u>age; sixt<u>y</u>, sixt<u>i</u>eth.

Exceptions: **1.** Keep the *y* before -*ing* and -*ist*
drying, replying, copying, copyist.

2. shyly, shyness, slyly, slyness, dryness, beauteous (but dryly or drily).

3. people's names: as in "the Kellys".

Following a vowel, final *y* is normally kept

pay, payable, payment; prey, preys, preyed; boys, boyish; joyful, joyous; buyer, buying.

Exceptions: paid, unpaid, laid, mislaid, said, slain, daily, gaily, gaiety.

Make a list of these words, close your book, and write correctly spelt new words formed from them by adding the suffix shown:

buoy, comply, defy, delay, display, flay, fry, imply, mortify, multiply, play, ply, pray, prey, pry, relay, reply, spray (+ *ed*).

ally, buoy, buy, comply, defy, obey, ply, replay, reply, vary (+ *ing*).

busy, dirty, fussy, grey, multiply, pray, pretty, silly, worry (+ *er*).

deny, duty, envy, justify, pity, play, ply, rely, vary (+ *able*).

betray, deny, try (+ *al*).

glory, joy, luxury, penury, victory (+ *ous*).

carry, marry (+ *age*).

ally, comply, dally, defy, vary (+ *ance*).

Silent -e

Keep the -e   before a suffix that begins with a consonant
love, loves, lovely; hate, hateful; safe, safety.
Exceptions: argue, argument; awe, awful; due, duly; nine, ninth; true, truly; whole, wholly.

Drop the -e   before a suffix that begins with a vowel
ic(e)+ed = iced; ow(e)+ing = owing;
haze, hazy; ache, aching; desire, desirous; mature, maturity.
Exceptions:

   Keep the -e   where the base word ends in -*ce* or -*ge* **and** the suffix begins with *a* or *o*
this keeps the *c* or *g* soft before the *a* or *o*
e.g. noticeable, manageable, courageous.

   Keep the -e   when adding -*ing*
if the base word ends in -*ee*, -*oe* or -*ye*
e.g. seeing, agreeing, decreeing, hoeing, shoeing, canoeing, eyeing, queueing
(but **not** in pursue, pursuing; ensue, ensuing).

   Keep the -e   in dye, singe, tinge
this distinguishes dyeing   singeing
from   dying   singing.

   Change the -e to *i* when adding -*al*, -*ous*
to certain base words ending in -*ce*
caprice   race   grace   vice
capricious racial   gracious vicious.

Make lists of these words, close your book, and write correctly spelt new words formed from them by adding the suffix shown:

agree, argue, become, die, dine, dye, judge, menace, page, pierce, pursue, queue, separate, serve, shoe, slope, sue, write (+ *ing*).

caprice, fame, grieve, nerve, outrage, prestige, space (+ *ous*).

believe, bridge, change, conceive, defence, deplore, desire, excuse, like, peace, remove, reverse, service (+ *able* or *ible*).

bare, complete, due, separate, sole, sparse, true, whole (+ *ly*).

approve, dispose, peruse, race, refuse, remove, reverse (+ *al*).

coincide, cohere, contrive, ignore, emerge, guide, resemble, revere, solve, subside, urge (+ *ance*, or + *ence*, or + *ency*).

Final Consonant – when to **double** it, and when **not** to.

The *p* in *hop* is doubled, when *-ing* is added, to make *hopping*. Yet the *m* in *seem* is not doubled in the word *seeming*.

The difference is that in *hop* the *p* has only **one** vowel in front of it, while in *seem* the *m* has **two**.

The *r* in *confer* is doubled in *conferring*, yet the *r* in *offer* is not doubled in the word *offering*.

The difference is that, in *conferring*, the *r* is in the **stressed** syllable of the word, while in *offered* the *r* is in an unstressed syllable.

The rule that governs these differences is:

double the final consonant of the base word if

1. it is a single consonant, and
2. there is only a **single** vowel in front of it, and
3. the suffix to be added begins with a vowel, and,
4. (where the base word has **two** or more syllables), the final syllable of the base word is the syllable that is stressed in pronouncing the *new* word.

Examples:

Single syllable base words:

bag, ba**gg**-age; beg, be**gg**-ar; fat, fa**tt**-est; red, re**dd**-ish;
ma**dd**-en, ro**bb**-ed, scra**pp**-ing; si**nn**-er, spo**tt**-ed, wi**tt**-y.

Longer base words (stressed syllable in bold type):

be**gin**	oc**cur**	for**bid**	for**get**
be**ginn**-er	oc**curr**-ed	for**bidd**-en	for**gett**-able
be**ginn**-ing	oc**curr**-ence	for**bidd**-ing	for**gett**-ing.

Note the effect of the position of the stress in:

con**fer**	de**fer**	pre**fer**	per**mitt**-ed
con**ferr**-ing	de**ferr**-ing	pre**ferr**-ing	e**lic**it-ed
confer-ence	**def**er-ent	**pre**fer-able	**ben**efit-ed.
al**lott**ed	ac**quitt**ed	e**quipp**ing	for**gett**able
balloted	**lim**ited	**gall**oping	**mark**etable.

Note that both **transfer*a*ble** and transfe**rri**ble are correct, and base words ending in *-our* drop the *u* before *-ous*, but not before *-able*:

glamour, glamorous; humour, humorous; honour, honourable.

Exceptions:

1. The final *-s* is not doubled in *gas-es*, but is doubled in
gass-ing, gass-ify.

2. When the suffix *-ic* is added, final consonants are not doubled: atomic, acidic, botanic, poetic, systemic.

3. A final *-c* is not doubled, but when a suffix beginning with *e* or *i* is added to the words *mimic, picnic, traffic*, the *c* is supplemented with a '*k*' to keep the hard sound of the *c*:
mimicked, picnickers, trafficking.

4. A final *w, x* or *y* is never doubled, e.g. saw-ing, tax-ation.

5. Where *-l* is the final consonant, the stress rule is ignored, and final *-l* is doubled in unstressed syllables, e.g.
quarrelled, towelling, travellers, libellous, revelling.
Exceptions: paralleled, parallelogram, scandalous, and **do not** double final *-l* before *-ise*, *-ism, -ist, -ity, -ize*, e.g. civil-ise, evangel-ist, formal-ity, imperial-ist, real-ism
(but due*ll*ist and meda*ll*ist do double the *-l*).

6. The words *kidnap, handicap* and *worship* do not follow the stress rule either, and the final *-p* is doubled in unstressed syllables in these words:
kidnapped, kidnapper; handicapped, handicapping; worshipper, worshipping.

Say why the final consonant of the base word is not doubled in the following cases:
act-or, sail-or, bow-ing, toil-ing, loud-ness, neat-est, reveal-ed, refrain-ing, exceed-ed, instalment, derail-ed.

Make a list of these words, close your book, and write correctly spelt new words formed from them by adding the suffix shown:
develop, garden, jewel, murder, picnic, propel, traffic, scan (+ *er*).

comb, envelop, favour, parallel, quit, remit, snub, trim (+ *ed*).

envelop, expel, handicap, instal, mimic, reveal, worship (+ *ing*).

covet, danger, glamour, humour, libel, marvel, pomp, scandal (+ *ous*).

actual, civil, moral (+ *ity*).

humour, journal, medal, novel (+ *ist*).

bear, favour, honour, prefer, sever, suffer, suit, transfer (+ *able*).

Same Sound – Different Spelling

Words

The English language includes many pairs and trios of words which sound the same but are spelt differently. See pages 57, 58 for over a hundred examples. One simply has to learn which word is spelt which way, using a dictionary if necessary.

Licence and *practice* (nouns) are often confused with *license* and *practise* (verbs), and *prophecy* (noun) with *prophesy* (verb). Remember the difference is the same as between *advice* (noun) and *advise* (verb): your ear will tell you the verbs have the *s*.

Be sure you do not confuse these spellings:

they're	short for "they are"		*it's*	short for "it is"
their	belonging to them		*its*	belonging to it
there	in that place			(no apostrophe)
you're	short for "you are"		*who's*	short for "who is"
your	belonging to you		*whose*	belonging to whom
no	the opposite of yes		*NOES*	those voting NO
know	be aware		*nose*	part of the face

Syllables

The syllables *-cede*, *-ceed* and *-sede* are often confused. It helps to remember that *supersede* is the only word with the *-sede* spelling; *exceed*, *proceed* and *succeed* are the only words with the *-ceed* spelling. All the rest – *concede*, *precede*, *recede*, etc. – have the *-cede* spelling.

Mistakes are often made with the endings *-cal* and *-cle*. The adjectives end in *-cal* and the nouns in *-cle*. Remember one of the *nouns* (names for *things*) is *article*. Some of the adjectives are: *clerical*, *magical*, *musical*, *physical*, *practical*. Some of the nouns are *article*, *bicycle*, *circle*, *obstacle*, *spectacle*, *vehicle*.

Similarly *principal* (ending in *-al*) is the adjective and *principle* the noun. (*Principal* is a noun when it is used of the head of a college, but it obtained this meaning only because of its adjectival sense, the Principal being the *top* member of staff).

Vowel Sounds

The following list shows how a single individual vowel sound may be spelt in a
dozen different ways:

Sound of	As in	Examples of other spellings of the same sound
a	bat	h<u>a</u>ve, s<u>a</u>lmon
a	bath	<u>au</u>nt, h<u>ea</u>rt, cl<u>e</u>rk, baz<u>aa</u>r, p<u>a</u>lm, hurr<u>ah</u>
a	bathe	n<u>a</u>tion, t<u>ai</u>l, pr<u>ay</u>, camp<u>aig</u>n, str<u>aig</u>ht, b<u>ea</u>r, r<u>ei</u>ns, th<u>ey</u>, r<u>eig</u>n w<u>eig</u>h, th<u>ere</u>, g<u>ao</u>l, g<u>au</u>ge, <u>eh</u>, d<u>ah</u>lia
e	bet	h<u>ea</u>d, s<u>ai</u>d, s<u>ay</u>s, l<u>eo</u>pard, l<u>ei</u>sure, <u>a</u>ny, fri<u>e</u>nd, Th<u>a</u>mes, b<u>u</u>ry
e	me	th<u>e</u>me, s<u>ee</u>n, <u>ea</u>ch, f<u>ie</u>ld, s<u>ei</u>ze, k<u>ey</u>, C<u>ae</u>sar, pol<u>i</u>ce, qu<u>ay</u>, p<u>eo</u>ple, B<u>eau</u>champ, <u>Oe</u>dipus
i	bit	pr<u>e</u>tty, b<u>ui</u>ld, w<u>o</u>men, s<u>ie</u>ve, g<u>i</u>ve, l<u>y</u>ric, b<u>u</u>sy
i	idle	m<u>i</u>ne, s<u>ig</u>n, h<u>ig</u>h, h<u>eig</u>ht, d<u>ie</u>, <u>i</u>sland, <u>ai</u>sle, <u>eye</u>, tr<u>y</u>, ind<u>i</u>ct, l<u>y</u>re, d<u>ye</u>, ch<u>oi</u>r
o	cot	sh<u>o</u>ne, w<u>a</u>nt, l<u>au</u>rel, kn<u>ow</u>ledge, y<u>a</u>cht, c<u>ou</u>gh
au	haul	l<u>aw</u>, t<u>a</u>ll, t<u>a</u>lk, <u>ough</u>t, <u>aug</u>ht, br<u>oa</u>d, V<u>aug</u>han
o	hero	foll<u>ow</u>, her<u>oe</u>s, follow<u>ed</u>, furl<u>oug</u>h
o	note	b<u>o</u>th, t<u>oa</u>d, t<u>oe</u>, d<u>oug</u>h, m<u>ow</u>, br<u>oo</u>ch, <u>oh</u>, y<u>eo</u>man, s<u>ew</u>, C<u>o</u>ckburn
oo	foot	c<u>ou</u>ld, w<u>o</u>lf
oo	fool	t<u>o</u>mb, sh<u>oe</u>, m<u>o</u>ve, s<u>ou</u>p, thr<u>ough</u>, tr<u>u</u>th, j<u>ui</u>ce, r<u>u</u>de, bl<u>ue</u>, sl<u>eu</u>th, sl<u>ew</u>, man<u>oeu</u>vre
u	shut	bl<u>oo</u>d, s<u>o</u>n, c<u>o</u>me, t<u>ou</u>ch, d<u>oe</u>s
u	duke	d<u>u</u>ty, d<u>ue</u>, s<u>ui</u>t, f<u>ew</u>, f<u>eu</u>d, l<u>ieu</u>, v<u>iew</u>, imp<u>u</u>gn, <u>ewe</u>, <u>you</u>, <u>yew</u>
oi	coin	b<u>oy</u>, b<u>uoy</u>, c<u>oig</u>n
ou	loud	d<u>ow</u>n, b<u>ow</u>ed, b<u>oug</u>h, McL<u>eo</u>d
any *vowel*	unstressed syllables	c<u>a</u>pacity, Sar<u>ah</u>, beach<u>es</u>, guin<u>ea</u>, forf<u>ei</u>t, terri<u>er</u>, hurri<u>ed</u>, tort<u>oise</u>, c<u>o</u>mmand, Eur<u>o</u>pe, thor<u>oug</u>hly, cupb<u>oa</u>rd, hum<u>our</u>, h<u>u</u>rrah, pleas<u>ure</u>, b<u>u</u>ry, monk<u>ey</u>.
	before an *r*	h<u>er</u>, h<u>ear</u>d, b<u>ir</u>d, st<u>ir</u>red, w<u>or</u>d, c<u>o</u>lonel, b<u>ur</u>st, bl<u>ur</u>red.

Phrasal Verbs

Component Parts

Many phrases consisting of a verb and either an adverb or a preposition have meanings of their own not easily deduced from the separate meanings of the two words used in the phrase. Thus we use the phrase *to give up* in the sense of *to cease*, e.g. "I must *give up* smoking", without intending any idea of *giving* or *upward* direction.

In some cases the meaning of at least one of the words used is still apparent in the meaning of the phrase, e.g. "I shall *write up* a full account", where the word *write* still means what it says, but the word *up* means *completely*.

In some cases the same phrase may have two meanings, e.g. "You *take on* (i.e. undertake) too much." "Don't *take on* so (i.e. take offence so easily)."

Sometimes a phrase of this kind is simply metaphorical, e.g. "I confessed because I was *leant on*" (i.e. subjected to threats).

Some such phrasal verbs may include more than one adverb or preposition, e.g. "I can't *put up with* (i.e. suffer) this noise."

Some verbs, especially one-syllable verbs, are used in this way with a great variety of adverb or preposition particles, as they are called.

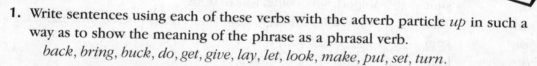

Exercises   on Phrasal Verbs

1. Write sentences using each of these verbs with the adverb particle *up* in such a way as to show the meaning of the phrase as a phrasal verb.
   back, bring, buck, do, get, give, lay, let, look, make, put, set, turn.

2. Write sentences showing the meaning of the phrasal verbs formed by adding the particles shown to the following verbs:

break	– *down, into, off, out*	go	–	*against, ahead,*
bring	– *about, in, off, on,*			*along with, at, by, for,*
	round, to			*on, on about, over, with*
call	– *off, on, out*	keep	–	*back, in with, on, on at*
carry	– *off, on, out*	knock	–	*about, back, down, off*
come	– *about, across, by, in for,*	lay	–	*in, into, off, on*
	into, of, off, round, to,	look	–	*after, out*
	upon	make	–	*for, off, out, up for*
do	– *away with, down, for,*	put	–	*off, on, out, up with*
	in, out of, without	set	–	*in, off, out*
get	– *about, around, at, on,*	stand	–	*by, for, in, out, up for*
	on to, over, up to	take	–	*after, in, off, on, to, up*
give	– *away, in, out, over*	turn	–	*down, in, on, out, to*